Miracles
of Rare
Device

Merlin and
Vivien

Miracles of Rare Device

The Poet's Sense of Self

in Nineteenth-Century Poetry

FRED KAPLAN

Queens College of the City University of New York

WAYNE STATE UNIVERSITY PRESS, DETROIT 1972

Published simultaneously in Canada by the
Copp Clark Publishing Company
517 Wellington Street, West Toronto 2B, Canada.

Grateful acknowledgment is made to the following for permission to quote or reproduce their works:
Wallace Stevens, *The Collected Poems of Wallace Stevens*. New York: Alfred A. Knopf, Inc., 1954.
Trustees of the Lady Lever Art Gallery, Port Sunlight, England.
Ernest Lee Tuveson, *The Imagination as a Means of Grace: Locke and the Aesthetics of Romanticism*. Berkeley: University of California, 1960.
The following chapters have been previously published in slightly different form. Grateful acknowledgment is made to the publishers for permission to include them here:
    Chapter 2 originally appeared as " 'The Tyger' and Its Maker. Blake's Vision of Art and the Artist" in *Studies in English Literature*, 7, no. 4 (Autumn 1967): 617-627.
    Chapter 6 originally appeared as "Tennyson's Merlin as Fallen Artist" in *Victorian Poetry*, 7 (1969): 285-298.

Library of Congress Cataloging in Publication Data

Kaplan, Fred, 1937-
    Miracles of rare device.

    Includes bibliographical references.
    1 English poetry—19th century—History and criticism.   2. Anxiety in litera-
ture.   I. Title.
PR585.A5K3   821'.7'09   73-38818
ISBN O-8143-1476-7

c C

To Gloria

"NOT
 IDEAS
 ABOUT
 THE THING
 BUT
 THE
 THING
 ITSELF"

Contents

1

From Blake to Browning

THIS IS A study of the structure and imagery of some major poems of the late eighteenth and the first half of the nineteenth centuries. Historical and cultural elements are considered only in so far as individual poems demand. The evidence is textual and suggestive, an experiment in critical reading, to support my premise that a major key to Romantic poetry is an understanding of how the artist reveals in his poetry his concern with himself as artist and with his art. Though a poetry of "the act of the mind" can best be complemented by analyses that respect the uniqueness of each such act, each chapter should be viewed as a selective variation on a single theme. Any value of this study derives partly from the assumption that great poems demand individual and intensive consideration

11

and partly from the importance of the pervasive theme which has played such a significant role in the tradition of western poetry.

The greatest achievements of Romantic poetry are in the short poem or in sections of larger ones. The Romantic epic endures mainly as a demonstration that the Romantics' epic ambitions far outpaced their achievements, and that their objective, heroic subjects were subverted by their subjective involvement with themselves as poets—as if they could write epics about writing epics.[1] They could not, and the dominant Romantic forms become the ode, the ballad,[2] and the variable lyric,[3] in which the relationship between the poet, his poetry, and his sense of his own creativity is a major topic. More often than not, for both the Romantic and the Victorian poet, it is the loss of his feeling of creativity that occupies him most:

> Men are more given to writing poems, especially love lyrics, in youth than in age. But it would seem that the classical poet was not afflicted with apprehension that his ability to write heroic poems of great theme would fade away. . . . In the romantic period the order is turned upside down. Many a romantic poet is haunted by the fear that the delicate adjustment of the nerves, the mechanism of keen emotional response that is the organ of imagination, must, like any other function of the body, begin to lose its vigor when youth is past. . . . It would seem that poets are fated to decline into critics; and critical analysis is fatal to real imaginative response.[4]

Even when the major Victorians turn to narrative and monolog these same concerns appear. This is so much the case that when the poet discovers a genre in which the long poem has promise again, when the poet becomes novelist as Byron does in *Don Juan* and Browning in *The Ring and the Book*, or romancer as Tennyson in *Idylls of the King*, this self-reflexive preoccupation still dominates. Thus the concern becomes a permanent and self-consciously manifested part of the poetic scene. Indeed, the legitimacy of the poet's involvement with himself as poet and with the creative process within the structure and the imagery of his poems, stressed by

Wordsworth in *The Prelude*, is validated in our own century by Wallace Stevens and others who have demonstrated that the poet's major preoccupation is with the poet, the poem, and their symbols:

> *The actor is*
> *A metaphysician in the dark, twanging*
> *An instrument, twanging a wiry string that gives*
> *Sounds passing through sudden rightness, wholly*
> *Containing the mind, below which it cannot descend,*
> *Beyond which it has no will to rise.*
>   *It must*
> *Be the finding of a satisfaction, and may*
> *Be of a man skating, a woman dancing, a woman*
> *Combing. The poem of the act of the mind.*
>   ("Of Modern Poetry")[5]

The larger purpose of my study, then, is to affirm the self-conscious poem of "the act of the mind" as an important phase in the poetic tradition.

Eleven major poems of the period have been chosen for close discussion: Blake's "The Tyger" (1790), Wordsworth's "Tintern Abbey" (1798), Coleridge's "Frost at Midnight" (1798) with minor glances at "Dejection: An Ode" (1802), Tennyson's "Locksley Hall" (1842) and "Merlin and Vivien" (1856), Arnold's "Empedocles on Etna" (1852), and Browning's "Andrea del Sarto" (1855), "Pictor Ignotus" (1845), "Dis Aliter Visum" (1864), and "Saul" (1845–1855). Though not each receives the same measure of attention, these eleven have been chosen because they are both major and representative, significant independent achievements and important topoi in the nineteenth-century's confrontation with the relationship between creative anxiety and the vehicle through which that anxiety is communicated. Each is evidence that between 1790 and 1864, among major poets, there was a gradually intensifying loss of faith in the power of poetry and creativity.[6]

Other poems might have found their appropriate place in this framework, particularly Keats's "Ode to a Nightingale," Coleridge's "Kubla Khan," Wordsworth's "Ode," and Shelley's "Ode to the West Wind" and "To a Skylark." They too are poems about the anxieties of their creators concerning their powers of creativity and their poems. But my approach is thematic. Where I have had the opportunity to choose between two poems that both basically serve the same function in my discussion, small gains and losses have been weighed, including how often and how successfully a particular poem has been treated critically. These omissions, of course, have permitted the Victorians to be brought into focus. At times something as undemonstrable but as important as personal preference has tipped the scales. Coleridge's "Dejection" and Browning's "Andrea del Sarto" tell basically the same tale of purgatorial neutrality that Keats tells in "Ode to a Nightingale." Coleridge's "dull pain / A grief without a pang, void, dark, and drear," depicts virtually the same state as Keats's "drowsy numbness" which "pains" his "sense." The end of feeling for poets who value feeling above all else is a state of partial death that can be expressed only in the most severe emotional terms, for the end of feeling is the end of poetry. For Keats, the fruitless pursuit of a poetry that he cannot realize, symbolized by the nightingale, emphasizes his sense of the comparative insignificance of his achievement. For Coleridge, the child of "Frost at Midnight," in contrast to the poet, represents the gap between the reality of the unfulfilled immediate self and the expectations of fulfillment. In a sense, "Frost at Midnight" and "Dejection: An Ode," taken together, cover much of the same ground as "Ode to a Nightingale," even to the verbal and emotional parallels between Keats's "bell / To toll me back from thee to my sole self" and Coleridge's "old church tower . . . bells" and "stern preceptor's face."

Shelley's "west wind" carries the same hope of poetic revitalization that comes on the breath of Wordsworth's "correspondent breeze" in its earlier analogs of landscape, memory, and love in "Tintern Abbey." In "To Wordsworth," a poem in which he deplores the political apostasy that he himself never lived to confront and to be tempted by, Shelley emphasizes his co-feeling with Wordsworth in regard to the things "which never may return: / Childhood and youth, friendship and love's first glow," and consequently associates himself with all the implied and expressed fears of loss of creativity that dominate the best of Wordsworth's poetry.

Like Wordsworth, Shelley almost is able to work out within the metaphors and the structure of his poems a formula for potential salvation, a breeze of hope and rebirth, of the poetic powers reviving and reascending. The great creative force, the west wind, "from whose solid atmosphere / Black rain, and fire, and hail will burst," so like the tumultuous cleansing storms of Coleridge's "Dejection" and Tennyson's "Merlin and Vivien," is analogue of the poet's own creativity. The west wind is Shelley's version of Coleridge's "articulate sounds of things to come," "the trumpet of a prophecy." Whereas, for Shelley, the total identification of the poetic self with this mysterious power represented by the west wind does not challenge the existence of the self, for Keats, of course, the threat remains that to this "high requiem" he may "become a sod." For the "fancy" is a "deceiving elf" that "cannot cheat so well / As she is fam'd to do." Wordsworth, not Coleridge or Keats, is surely Shelley's master and kindred spirit. They share a mood and a conviction, a sense of confidence in their poetic missions and in the powers of poetry, that make "To a Skylark" almost as secure an expression of this confidence as "Tintern Abbey." Like Wordsworth, who transforms a landscape that never was, a landscape of the imagination, Shelley transforms his "bird that never wert" into an emblem of the perfect poet without revealing any deeply troubled sense of a major gap between the emblem's powers and his own.

Historically, Blake begins the tradition of self-exploration with what is a triumphantly unself-conscious expression of the expansion of his consciousness and a celebration of his limitless powers as a poet. Browning concludes it with a dispirited depiction of a self-conscious and powerless failed poet, "famous," however, "for verse or worse," the egocentric poet manqué of "Dis Aliter Visum" whose date of 1864 marks the forward boundary of this study. Browning's poet is the extreme point of contrast in self-consciousness and sense of failure, at least chronologically, with Blake's successful creator and creation in "The Tyger." However, as one moves backward from 1864 to Tennyson's Merlin, Arnold's Empedocles, and Coleridge's "aeolian lute / Which better far were mute," there is no substantial decrease in sense of concern for loss of poetic power and mission.

2

Blake's Artist

LIKE A MIRACULOUS sponge, Blake's "The Tyger" has absorbed many interpretations without becoming waterlogged. Appreciators of the poem have contrasted the tiger with the lamb, experience with innocence, the behemoth and albatross created by some wondrous nature or god in his unquestionable wisdom. Critics of the poem have explored Blake's use of irony and dramatic characterization, seeing the tiger as the pussy-cat creation of a braggart Nobodaddy. Still other Blakeans have studied the text of the poem, its revisions, its historical implications, its occult symbols, and its position in the structure of Blake's developed mythology.[1]

The central problem that critics of the poem must face, and often have, can be reduced conveniently to the question, "Who made the tiger?" The solution often depends upon the answer to another query, "What qualities characterize this particular tiger?" In a special sense, Blake himself as artist (not Nobodaddy or Urizen or Nature) created the tiger, and this tiger's major characteristics are those of the work of art as conceived by Blake during the writing of *Songs of Experience*. The poem is as much about the relationship between the artist as creator and the work of art as creation, as about man's view of the relationship between the general creator of things and one of the things he has created.[2] The tiger is, among other things, *this* poem in particular and in general all those works of art that represent a formalization of "the forests of the night," the world of experience and nature. The hand or eye that framed this "fearful symmetry" is Blake's specifically and that of the shaper of experience into artistic forms universally.

The tiger seems as symbolic as the rose, the sunflower, the lily, the clod, the pebble, and the other explicitly physical items from the world of nature in *Songs of Experience*. Though the beast must be visualized initially as a literal tiger, the effectiveness of the poem derives from Blake's creation of a tiger so unusual both in itself and in relation to its maker that literal visualization fails to account for the poem. Nevertheless, the effect of the poem's first two words is to evoke a vivid picture of a conventional tiger.[3] While part of the visualization may involve leonine grace and beauty, certainly most readers, responding to the repetition, would associate the tiger with more than human power and forcefulness. Both in the terms of our society and in Blakean terms, there is nothing inherently evil about a tiger: that its symmetry is fearful and its terrors deadly describe the potentiality of its strength rather than the result of its destructiveness. The tiger is in no way morally or ethically reprehensible, is, in fact, no more subject to the restricting moral codes of institutions and reason than is the poet of *The Marriage of Heaven and Hell* who says that "those who restrain desire, do so because theirs is weak enough to be restrained." The restraint placed upon the tiger is ultimately the form that its maker gives it, in the same way that the formal structure of the poem "The Tyger" is the restraint that Blake places upon his imaginative conception. This kind of limitation is the price of creation.

The repetition of the word "tyger" in the poem's first and sixth stanzas not only suggests the power of the animal but anticipates the seemingly simplistic tone of wonder that pervades all six stanzas. The initial repetition of "Tyger! Tyger" anticipates the repetition of the entire first stanza in the last stanza, a kind of "fearful symmetry" itself in which the poem's beginning and end are almost identical expressions, holding between them four stanzas of questions in which rhetoric, irony, and wonder are mixed in unequal proportions, the latter predominating. That the first and the last stanza ask a single almost identical question, and the middle four stanzas a series of questions, emphasizes that we are dealing with characteristics and actions so ritualistic and talismanic that the repetition only increases their awesomeness. In terms of punctuation and syntax, not to speak of semantic characteristics, from the opening words and throughout the poem this tiger is indeed a miraculous creature.

That the tiger is burning brightly need not be understood in any special Blakean sense, except to the degree that Blake himself makes use of the traditional association between fire and creativity, between the furnace-forge and the creating imagination. In a process of transference, that which is a product of the creative fire itself burns, as the burning bush burns—continuously—as a vehicle to embody and convey the divine presence. If this burning were a form of catharsis or purification, surely Blake would have found some way to suggest the termination or at least the result of this purgation, whereas the tense form indicates a continuous fire and the repetition of the same phrase in the final stanza of the poem emphasizes that the intervening four stanzas have in no way exhausted the tiger's fuel. The way in which the tiger burns is not the way "whate'er is born of mortal birth" burns in "To Tirzah":

> *Whate'er is born of mortal birth*
> *Must be consumed with the earth.*

This tiger is no more consumed than is the burning bush.

Though there have been valiant attempts to locate "the forests of the night," none have been totally successful. Blake's illustration for the poem, reproduced and discussed by John E. Grant in his "The Art and Argument of 'The Tyger,' " includes part of a rather stark, barren tree to the left of which stands the beast. Grant suggests that "this tree of Death epitomizes the fallen or vegetable world; it represents the forests of the night. . . ." [4] Neither the first line of the poem nor the poem as a whole nor the drawing of the tree supports the first assertion; however, the second is a reasonable guess at the relationship Blake intended between the poem and the illustration. The topographical relationship between the tiger and the forest in the poem is represented visually by the two main images of the illustration, the tiger and the tree. Perhaps the single tree represents the world of single vision that Blake in another place calls upon God to keep us from: "single vision and Newton's sleep." For this world of single vision that "the forests of the night" may represent, that the tiger inhabits at the moment of its initial introduction into the poem and at the moment of its final appearance in the poem's last stanza, is a cluttered and ambiguous world, the world of nature, consequently "forests," and a world without essential clarity, hence, "of the night." It is the world from which the maker draws the material to shape the tiger. It is the world to which the maker will return his creation. The tiger, "burning bright," is the clarified and unambiguous product of the artist's imagination, taking its substance from the disordered real world and existing as an art product in that world, that is, "in the forests of the night." Succinctly, "the forests of the night" represent the material the artist has not shaped imaginatively into the clarity and light of artistic form. The tiger, then, symbolizes artistic form. The single tiger shines like a bright light against a dark background.

Except for the substitution of "dare" for "could," the first question of the poem:

> *What immortal hand or eye*
> *Could frame thy fearful symmetry?*

is also its final question. Both by positioning and meaning, these almost identical queries are central to the effectiveness of the poem. If the tiger *is* this poem specifically and universally all those works of art that represent a formalization of "the forests of the night," of the world of experience, then the hand or eye that framed this "fearful symmetry" is Blake's in particular and the artist's in general. Whereas in *Songs of Innocence* Blake uses, often with bitter irony, the materials of the world of the lamb as the subject matter of his work of art, in *Songs of Experience* he uses the materials of the world of the tiger, the "forests of the night," both as subject matter and, when shaped into the "fearful symmetry" of the tiger, as symbolic representative of the type of poem that is the product of visualizing this world. I suggest that Blake, struck by the strength of his imaginative conception of the tiger, and anticipating the powerful vision that the poem would embody, writes in the fourth line not of the "fearful symmetry" of the literal tiger but of the "fearful symmetry" of the tiger as this specific poem and as a symbol of the poems of *Songs of Experience*.

That the "hand or eye" that framed the tiger is an immortal one should come as no surprise to readers of Blake and does not contradict the equating of the tiger's creator with Blake himself. For Blake, not only is "everything that lives . . . holy," but everything that lives on the human level is potentially immortal through the exercise of the imagination.[5] In the Blakean ontology, God becomes man to the extent that man becomes God. Man's rise to divinity, or, more accurately, his attempt to regain the shape and substance of his partially lost or reduced divinity, is directly dependent upon his use of his imagination. Man becomes God when man extends his imagination to create, out of the raw materials of experience, the work of art that transcends the world of experience. The answer, then, to the first question of the poem, "Who made the tiger," is first Blake, then the artist, then man. Blake as artist could create the tiger. Blake as artist, extending his imagination, could expand the god-like within himself, could, in effect, be immortal. Like the tiger, the maker of the tiger is wondrous to behold. Blake the artist does not fear to recognize his immortality; in fact, he stands in awe before his own fearlessness.

The reader who has followed thus far can anticipate the pattern, if not the details, of the remainder of this explication of "The Tyger."

> *In what distant deeps or skies*
> *Burnt the fire of thine eyes?*

may refer either to the eyes of the tiger, especially since it is the
tiger who has been "burning" in the first stanza, or to the eyes that
are the visualizing and conceptualizing agents of the body, or, more
accurately, of the imagination, to which belong also the "immortal
hand or eye" that "could frame thy fearful symmetry." The direct
address of the query indicates through the use of "thine" that the
voice of the poem is speaking to and of the tiger. But to settle for
this direct identification is to disregard some of the important com-
plexities of the poem. For example, most critics agree that the eye
image in Blake represents, among other things, "the shaping spirit
of imagination." [6] Certainly it represents this in line three. The
words "burn" and "fire" suggest the hot crucible of the creative
imagination. Blake often topographically mythologizes and creates
a place that is the crucible or forge of creation, as he does in the
poem's fourth stanza when he compares the process of creation to
the muscular efforts of the great smithy Vulcan pounding matter
into form in his hot furnace. Though the voice of the poem directly
addresses the tiger as art product in the second stanza, the tiger has
become associated inseparably with its maker the artist. The "eye"
of the third line of the first stanza is associated with the "eyes" of
the second stanza, emphasizing the relationship of maker to made,
he whose imagination is fire creating a product that burns.

The "distant deeps and skies" then would refer, like "the forests of the night," to the place in which the work of art exists, if it
were not for the change in tense. We have moved from the present
of "burning" to the past of "burnt." [7] Whereas in the first stanza,
as in the last, the art product is being described in its timeless and
forever present existence, the second stanza has begun referring in
the past tense to the same art product in its finite moment of creation. The four middle stanzas of the poem describe in the past
tense the activity of the artist and the developing characteristics of
his work of art during those particular moments of creation. The
final stanza, significantly, returns to the present tense. The "distant
deeps or skies" refer both to a place and a time: the place is a place

which Blake associates with the four states of existence, but the traditional furnace of creative activity, the imagination of the artist, in which the artist creates his awesome tiger.[13]

That a cosmic drama with theological overtones immediately follows Blake's description of the activities of a Vulcan-artist has puzzled many of the poem's critics. References to stars throwing down their spears and heaven being watered appear in later Blake poems, and perhaps the same special Blakean theological considerations apply to "The Tyger." But it is unnecessary to assume that Blake in approximately 1790 had worked out in specific detail his complicated mythology of man's fall to which he first makes detailed reference in *Vala or the Four Zoas*, the first draft of which was probably composed between 1795 and 1797.[14] It is sufficient to interpret these troublesome lines within the context of the poem itself. David Erdman, using the figure of "the creative blacksmith who seizes the molten stuff of terror and shapes it into living form on the cosmic anvil" to describe the artist of stanza four, suggests that the "stars throwing down their spears" is the direct result of the exertions of the blacksmith who "drives out the impurities in a shower of sparks, like the fallen stars children call angels' tears."[15] Here the exertions of the blacksmith directly cause the metaphorical heavenly downpour. It is plausible that by "the stars throwing down their spears" Blake meant to describe metaphorically the traditional heavenly phenomena that accompany an unusual occurrence or creation in the human world, such as the disturbances in nature that accompany the braggart Glendower's birth in *Henry IV*. The "stars throwing down their spears" could, of course, represent falling stars in the night sky. They would "water heaven with their tears" in the sense that heaven, the whole night sky, metaphorically is rained on by a shower of shooting or falling stars. Thus, the heavens respond to the fearlessness of the artist and the fearfulness of his creation.

The final questions of the fifth stanza:

> *Did he smile his work to see?*
> *Did he who made the Lamb make thee?*

emphasize the wonderfulness of the artist and his work of art. In both cases the answer to the question is yes. The "glittering eyes" of the artist "are gay," like those of Yeats's Chinamen in "Lapis Lazuli." That he smiles now with the joyfulness of a god who is beyond mortality and "the forests of the night" is no surprise, since he himself has become immortal through his actions as an artist. The final question, rhetorical and slightly ironic, asks, did he who made the poem "The Lamb" or the illustration for that poem also make the poem "The Tyger" or its illustration. Is the artist who created these two very different works of art the same man? Did the poet who could conceive of the work of art as an image of gentleness and pastoral beatitude also conceive of it as an image of fearful wonder and mental apocalypse? Since the voice of the poem is the voice of the poet, and the poet as visionary and man as God are responsible for all creation, this is hardly different from making a comment in the form of a question on creativity and creation in general.

Finally, Blake returns in the last stanza to the first, and the "fearful symmetry" of his work of art is complete. The single change from "could" to "dare" emphasizes the almost unbelievable boldness of the artist in daring to create something as fearful and as awesome as this poem and the *Songs of Experience*. As the series of questions develop, the answers become more and more obvious. The poem as a whole, then, is a series of rhetorical questions framed by an image that represents the work of art and an image that represents the world of experience, of nature, from which the work of art derives its subject matter and in which as artifact it exists. The ultimate answer to all the questions is Blake himself, or some surrogate for Blake, possibly Daedalus or Vulcan, or the sculptor, the artist in general, or the imagination of the artist, or even what the artist has created as something inseparable from the artist himself. Regardless of the surrogate, which supplies valuable modifications and extensions, the point is the same. The powers of the artist and his art are not only analogous to, they are identical to, the powers of creation in the universe of the imagination. Ultimately all creation is within the levels and developments of men's minds, their power simultaneously to see and to create. The maker of the tiger must also be the maker of all things, the maker of all things the maker of the tiger. But both are Blake. His visions are his creations. What the mind can imagine, that is real and existent; the act of imagining creates its reality. But for Blake the act of imagining involves words; the vision must have verbal expression. He then can see and express what most others cannot:

> I assert for My self that I do not behold the Outward Creation & that to me it is hindrance & not Action it is as the Dirt upon my feet No part of Me. What it will be Questioned When the Sun rises do you not see a round Disk of fire somewhat like a Guinea O no no I see an Innumerable company of the Heavenly host crying Holy Holy Holy is the Lord God Almighty I question not my Corporeal or Vegetative Eye any more than I would Question a Window concerning a Sight I look thro it & not with it.
>
> "A Vision of the Last Judgment"

The powers, then, of this poet are immense in his own eyes, his confidence in his creativity unshakeable.

Unlike the major Romantics and Victorians who became obsessed with self-conscious purposefulness about the artist and his powers and whose poems reflect the channeling of general concern about the universe at large into their more specialized anxiety, Blake had no difficulty in combining his general vision of creative power and creation in the universe at large with his vision of the role of the poet and poetry in this process. For Blake, all vision is the poet's prerogative, that is, the visionary must be a poet and the poet must be a visionary prophet. There is no gap or distinction between the creator of all things and his creation on the one hand, and the poet and his poem on the other. Of course, later in his career, through an astounding series of complex myths and metaphors, Blake was to dare to claim that man in some former prelapsarian form had authored all creation through his imaginative powers and that all that was needed for the revitalization of man's powers was an effort of will and expanding imagination. Obviously Blake intended his poems to be a series of leaps towards this revitalization, towards man's assumption of his deity again, and both the force and the place of such expansion was to be man's imagination. Ultimately, the "imagined land" was the real land and all "real" things, then, were within man's individual and collective imagination. For Blake, vision and creation were simultaneous. Consequently a poem about vision was also a poem about creation and the reverse. It hardly matters how self-conscious Blake was about the synthesis he had effected, except to note that obviously his confidence in his vision resulted in a degree of inner anxiety and self-reflexive doubt concerning his mission as visionary poet so considerably less than the rather extreme and self-conscious doubts felt by the other major Romantics, that he seems to have lived in a comparative paradise of unquestioned confidence in his powers.

Blake condemned Wordsworth for worshipping nature, though Wordsworth would not have condemned Blake for worshipping man. But only Wordsworth, and to a lesser extent Shelley, among the Romantics, and Browning, though rarely, among the Victorians, shared a portion of Blake's confidence in his mission. Each had a very different rationale for his assurance and comparative freedom from creative anxiety.

effect upon his readers very similar to the effect Wordsworth tells us nature has had upon him. Just as nature is to act as a vehicle of release from depression and a catalyst of positive affirmation, so too he seems to intend his poetry to be a vehicle of release and rebirth for his readers. In such a way, in fact, have Mill and others used Wordsworth's poetry, and though there is no external statement by Wordsworth himself on the subject, examination of the structure of "Lines Composed a Few Miles above Tintern Abbey, On Revisiting the Banks of the Wye during a Tour. July 13, 1798" supports this supposition.[2] As a totality, "Tintern Abbey" seems to exemplify how poets "from their native selves can send abroad / Kindred mutations" (*The Prelude*, XIV, ll. 93-94) to be for their readers the agents of revitalization and rebirth that "the power" of "Nature" has been for them.[3] Like Blake's tiger, Wordsworth's landscape and his poem are symbolic representations of the interaction between the artist and his art product, between the poem and its reader. Except for Shelley, of all the Romantics only Blake and Wordsworth managed any degree of confidence in the efficacy of their poetry. For Wordsworth, "Tintern Abbey" was not only a record of his own rebirth, but a structural and imagistic formula for the revitalization of all those who, like Coleridge, Keats, and Mill, have lost the "passion and the life, whose fountains are within." [4]

The opening of "Tintern Abbey" suggests the present sluggishness of the poet's spirit and imagination, summarizing his "five long" years of dependency upon memory for revitalization.[5] Shaping autobiography into myth, Wordsworth absorbs the fact of his absence from the lovely banks of the river Wye into his favorite fiction:[6] the complete absence of the poet from nature which is the partial source of his creative powers; his voluntary imprisonment in the devitalizing city; his dependency upon memory for renewal of creativity; the fading of his once vivid impressions of nature leading to depression and loss of faith in personal creativity; and his return to nature which catalyzes an affirmation of his creative powers that permits him once more to return to the city. Then, like *Finnegans Wake*, the story having been told, the story begins again.[7]

The landscape to which Wordsworth has returned somewhat resembles the landscape of Coleridge's "Kubla Khan," suggesting that, like Coleridge, he is writing a poem about poetry, the poet, and the creative process.[8] The stately opening of "Tintern Abbey" is paralleled by a similar opening in "Kubla Khan." The sacred river Alph, which suggests some primal river of poetic inspiration, is paralleled by the river Wye:

> *These waters, rolling from their mountain-springs*
> *With a soft inland murmur.*

Both rivers are calm, majestic; both come from some primal source of waters, the Wye from "mountain-springs," the Alph from "a mighty fountain [which] slanted / Down the green hill," and both are associated with the Romantic metaphor of mountains and springs as equivalents for the source within the poet of his imagination. Both poems make the frequent Romantic equation of rivers and streams with the flow of the imagination and the creative process.[9]

Wordsworth's poem, however, moves in a chronological and geographical sequence, while Coleridge's moves with visionary leaps. In "Kubla Khan," we leap from the stately Alph in the first section to the source of the river in the second without the assistance of ordinary connectives. In "Tintern Abbey," the myth imposes a more natural structure. The poet hears in the distance the "waters, rolling from their mountain-springs"; and, at that moment, he is in the presence of the "romantic chasm" that Coleridge describes in section two. But Wordsworth's "romantic chasm" combines the measured enclosures of human cultivation of Coleridge's first section with the "green hill athwart a cedarn cover" of the second. Having returned after five years of absence, Wordsworth creates a situation in which myth outweighs autobiography.[10] He sees before him the traditional Romantic landscape, which, as in the second section of "Kubla Khan," has elements that are "steep," "lofty," "wild," "secluded," "dark," "unripe"; as in the first, it is cultivated with unobtrusive imaginativeness:

> *These hedge-rows, hardly hedge-rows, little lines*
> *Of sportive wood run wild: these pastoral farms,*

> *Green to the very door; and wreaths of smoke*
> *Sent up, in silence, from among the trees!*
>
> (ll. 15-18)

Residing in this landscape are the wanderers, "vagrant dwellers," and, of course, the solitary hermit himself, one phase in the development of the Wordsworthian poet.

The solitary hermit of "Tintern Abbey" contrasts starkly with the narrator, the complete Wordsworthian poet. Deaf to humanity, he functions as a contrast to the poet who has heard "the still, sad music of humanity." The poet's role within Wordsworth's myth necessitates that he return, like Plato's Philosopher-King, from his vision of the forms of nature, Wordsworth's Platonic sun, to the affairs of men, Plato's cave.[11] Having withdrawn permanently into the "romantic chasm," forever developing and basking in the warmth of his imagination, the hermit suggests an aborted poet who has failed to involve himself in the relevant myth. Transforming this stock figure of eighteenth-century landscape literature,[12] Wordsworth tells us that the hermit is not an actual or particular person but lives in a world of seeming; that is, the rather illusory "wreaths of smoke" are

> *Sent up, in silence, from among the trees!*
> *With some uncertain notice, as might seem*
> *Of vagrant dwellers in the houseless woods,*
> *Or of some Hermit's cave, where by his fire*
> *The Hermit sits alone.*
>
> (ll. 18-22)

Rather than create a hermit with the reality of a fictional character, Wordsworth creates a hermit with the reality of metaphor. Permanent isolation of the poet or of the imagination in this primal landscape would reduce the poet to the non-reality, the *seeming* posture of the hermit. The poet must move through the successive stages of the Wordsworthian myth in a continuous process.

The first section of "Tintern Abbey," then, makes use of situations and metaphors that have their parallels in "Kubla Khan" and in other Romantic poems, suggesting that Wordsworth begins his poem as a veiled description of the creative process and of the more general life patterns of the poet. The myth of the creative process and of the function of the poet then presented is arranged in a structure which encourages in the reader an experience of progression from darkness and sterility to clarity and creativity, similar to what the poet ascribes to his own reading of nature. Through reading this poetic account of the process of rebirth, Wordsworth intends his reader to experience a similar revitalization. Wordsworth's aesthetic, then, is one that emphasizes reader participation and identification with moods and experiences that he believes all men share.[13] Poetry shall be redemptive in a therapeutic fashion for both poet and reader. By identifying our own "case" with his "case," by surrendering ourselves to the intricacies of his psychological movement, by giving ourselves to the structure, rhythm, and imagery of his poem, Wordsworth imagines that the story of his redemption will not only show us the way to our own but will effect it.

It is "these beauteous forms" now directly visible, but at most other times impressed upon the memory with an intensity that decreases as absence from them increases, which have provided "in lonely rooms . . . sweet sensations," moral models, and, most importantly, as the syntax indicates (ll. 35-49), a vehicle of emotional and psychological release or intensification which has caused the poet to see "into the life of things." It is the poet's "reading" of nature that is similar to the sensitive reader's "reading" of "Tintern Abbey." There are ideal images and patterns to correspond to the ideal forms of nature. Wordsworth's rhetoric and syntax make it clear that "sensations sweet," moral elevation, and visionary insight are to be the rewards which "nature's priest" is to share with the reader through the vehicle of the poem.[14]

In the first section of "Tintern Abbey," Wordsworth, consequently, manipulates Romantic imagery to plunge the reader into the mood of the long absent poet returning to a landscape of primal power. In the second, he manipulates syntax and sentence structure to create in the reader the very effect of ascending in "lonely rooms," through memories of nature, from depression and weariness, to joy, harmony, and visionary insight. In effect, lines 22-48 consist of two sentences, the connective "nor" knitting the two into an unusually close semantic and rhythmic unity, each split into two sections by the use of a colon and a dash after the words "restoration" and "lightened." The first of the four major clauses comments on the general significance of these "beauteous forms" and refers specifically to the first and perhaps least important of the gifts derived from the interaction of memory and landscape, the "sensations sweet felt in the blood." The second major clause, the remainder of the first sentence, presents with dramatic and rhythmic emphasis the second gift, the "feelings" that "influence" the "nameless, unremembered acts / Of kindness and of love." With the phrase "nor less, I trust, / To them I may have owed," Wordsworth refers back to the original subject, "these beauteous forms," summarizes their efficacy on the two levels already mentioned, and bridges his sentences without impeding the intensifying movement towards a climax. In fact, the movement is accelerated. The third clause mentions the third and most important of the gifts and begins the description of "that blessed mood" with which the rest of these lines are concerned. The tension is increased through anaphora until suddenly, and quite miraculously, Wordsworth leaps us across this boundary of rhythmic pause by repeating with some expansion the phrase from the third clause, "that blessed mood," in the initial position in the fourth major clause, "that serene and blessed mood." All this has *been* preparation for the vision which concludes this section of the poem:

> —that serene and blessed mood,
> In which the affections gently lead us on,—
> Until, the breath of this corporeal frame
> And even the motion of our human blood
> Almost suspended, we are laid asleep
> In body, and become a living soul:
> While with an eye made quiet by the power
> Of harmony, and the deep power of joy,
> We see into the life of things.
>
> (ll. 41-49)

Now the poet returns from his review of the myth in his memory to his present moment of depression and doubt.[15] Naturally, he returns to the river Wye, his symbol for the waters and the landscape that have never yet failed to provide rebirth. The movement from vision within memory to depression in the midst of symbolic landscape is accomplished by the manipulation of rhetoric and syntax. The use of an "if . . . yet" clause manages to affirm the vision while vividly depicting the suffering of the poet "in darkness." The division of the sentence creates a three part arrangement. The first clause, "If . . . oft," briefly presents the poet's uncertainty counterbalanced by a sudden memory of what this landscape has meant to him. The second clause, the pivot of the sentence, holds in suspension the vision of this landscape that has remained in his memory while it describes his condition of depression and loneliness in the city, to be echoed by Keats in "the weariness, the fever, and the fret." The final phrase in the clause semantically describes and rhythmically captures the sentence's overall movement up to this point: "Have hung upon the beatings of my heart." Wordsworth's reader, then, hangs at the brink of this movement, anticipating in the reference to the heart an amplified return to the first part of the sentence, the "sensations sweet felt in the blood." Anaphora, as it does so often, comes to Wordsworth's and the reader's rescue.[16] The final clause, following the closing of the parenthetical recall of past misery, returns to the "how oft" of the first clause, gathering up all the previous currents and bringing them to an emotional unity that is strengthened and made more complex by the return to the "oh" of line 50 in the "o" of line 56, by the variation of "how oft" (l. 50), "how oft" (l. 55) and then "how often" (l. 57), and the repetition of "turned to thee" in lines 55 and 57. The movement is an ascension, held back by a powerful negative tug from the past, but moved forward by a rising structure that will not be denied and by a half dozen subtle interweavings that force the reader to move into the present without letting go of the past. The movement insists upon continuity without stasis, and in its final effect is consolatory, moving the reader to a present in which he experiences consolation in the ever-present world of memory as well as in the immediacy of the poem's present tense.

One of the hardly noticed but key changing points in the poem develops directly out of Wordsworth's concentration upon the significance of the river Wye. For all his concentration on the artist's imagination and the important relationship between what is seen and what is half-created, Wordsworth will not accept an imagination and an art that does not connect the single and subjective poet to the objective world and human society.[17] The simple change from "have I turned to thee" (l. 55) to "has my spirit turned to thee" (l. 57) transforms a situation of personal ego release into one in which a force greater than the self, one's spirit or imagination, predominates, anticipating the humanistic liberation that is to climax the next verse stanza of the poem. The myth of the poet and the destiny of the poem require a constant though crucial movement from a state of liberation of the imagination to a state in which that imagination is humanized.[18]

The other two sections of the poem (ll. 58-111 and 112-159) recapitulate the ontology of the myth and project it forward to future recitations. The poet turns from the "sylvan Wye" flowing before his eyes to the river of his memory. He is at that point in the myth when the sensory impressions of nature embedded in his memory in the past have lost their sharp edges. But "the picture of the mind revives again" in a rebirth analogous to that of his own imagination, catalyzed by the pleasure the poet feels, knowing "that in this moment there is life and food / For future years." The efficacy of this process of replenishment has been affirmed only moments before when the five-year-old "picture of the mind revives again." The use of "so" to summarize the movement from the past to the present of the myth immediately before the present tense verb "I dare" in line 65 increases the emphasis on optical vision in the present that subsequently is to be reinforced by Wordsworth's description of the landscape before him, though almost concurrently he is drawn back into the scenes of the past.

The myth of the rebirth of the poet now finds its autobiographical analog in Wordsworth's youthful experiences with the undifferentiated continuum. Perhaps it would be more accurate to say that Wordsworth draws upon a version of his childhood experiences to demonstrate vividly the importance of rebirth through nature, or through the poem, while at the same time indicating that this experience is analogous to only one step in the myth of the poet and the creative process. The myth actually is a myth of time as well as of place. While the general patterns have an abstractness similar to that of Plato's allegory of the cave, the abstract pattern or mythic process is grounded in the literary specificity of autobiography. Often the autobiography borders on a "supreme fiction," and it is just this Wordsworthian manipulation of remembrances of childhood experiences, of a special insight and power that had been granted to him, combined with the comparatively impersonal myth of the poet and the creative process, that helps to create one of the dominant characteristics of Wordsworth's poetry: "profundity," objectivity, and universality on the one hand; naiveté, subjectivity, and emotional specificity on the other.[19]

But even the alleged autobiographical experience that underlies the statement of lines 58-85 has the reality of a literary document and a literary experience known both to the poet and to his readers in the words of the poem that gave it form and expression. In the "prelude" to the objective epic he was never to complete, Wordsworth had the singular distinction of writing a full-length version of what as an adult he believed his childhood experience not only meant but actually was.[20] Both in *The Prelude* and in "Tintern Abbey," Wordsworth exercises the poet's prerogative of creating a past that may never have been in order to create a formal pattern which absorbs and explains his experiences.

So much has been written about the theological implications of Wordsworth's poetic statements on nature that only recently has recognition been given to the non-theological, symbolic emphasis of landscape descriptions in Wordsworth's poetry and in nineteenth-century poetry in general. Wordsworth's nature, however, is not only sometimes apocalyptic and ambiguous, a veil behind which is to be seen both the tiger and the lamb, but it is also like Wallace Stevens's "ultimate elegance: the imagined land."[21] It is an artifice within an artifice, a set of cohesive symbols within a cohered unity. Wordsworth's admission, "I cannot paint / What then I was" (ll. 75-76), is not merely a rhetorical device, but a considered and truthful recognition of his practice of recreating the past to serve the needs of the present. The landscape of the past has been long forgotten; what is remembered is the "appetite; a feeling and a love" (l. 80). The need of the moment is to create a symbolic landscape that will represent the emotions he now believes he felt in his childhood experiences with nature. The distinction is important. The emphasis here is on the "half create" part of the phrase, "both what they half create / And what perceive" (ll. 106-107). And particularly vivid in the poet's imagination are "their colors and their forms" (l. 79), a distillation of the structural essence which points to the aesthetic rather than the theological foundation of Wordsworth's landscape.[22] The landscape that Wordsworth creates is very much like a Wordsworthian poem in which the colors and the forms are the emotional substance and the psychological structure, the images and their organization. Wordsworth's readers cannot separate his vision of nature from his vision of poetry.

The humanization of the visionary experience is presented next, as an essential development in the experience of the poet. Wordsworth sees in his own imagined life and imagined land the relevant example of the movement from the undifferentiated continuum to a humanized wisdom. The autobiographical example is model for the myth and catalyst for the poem, just as the process is the subject of the poem and nature is the agent of rebirth. "The still, sad music of humanity" suggests that the humanization of these visions is connected to some pattern of "music" or song, and that the ultimate embodiment of the stoic vision of the mature Wordsworth is within Wordsworthian poetry, which itself could be described aptly as

> The still, sad music of humanity,
> Nor harsh nor grating, though of ample power
> To chasten and subdue.
>
> (ll. 91-93)

It is difficult not to read this, as has not yet been done, as a comment by the author on his own poem and on the major poems of his future career. It is difficult not to read the remainder of this section of the poem, to the period in line 111, as further comment by Wordsworth on the inextricable relationship between nature and the poem, since the effect is to bring the reader to the climax of the myth as Wordsworth conceived it. The humanization of the imagination and nature has not destroyed their essential spirituality. Having moved from depression, relieved only by the weakening images of memory, to a renewed contact with the forms of nature, Wordsworth now at his moment of highest insight affirms the simultaneous existence of the human and superhuman within the poet. The mature poet returns to the cave with a humanized vision of the sun. The basic implications of his synthesized vision are moral and social:

> *well pleased to recognise*
> *In nature and the language of the sense*
> *The anchor of my purest thoughts, the nurse,*
> *The guide, the guardian of my heart, and soul*
> *Of all my moral being.*
>
> (ll. 107-111)

This moment of insight Wordsworth probably intends to be the reader's also because the imagery, the syntax, and the sentence structures have been manipulated to create within the reader a strong sense of the ultimate maturity of this synthesis of man and nature, of humanity and spirituality, of poet and poem. The "dizzy raptures" give way to "the round ocean and the living air." Anaphoric techniques, combined with a careful selection of vowel patterns and sentence structures, force the reader to move with slow seriousness, emphasizing the coalescence of subject matter with process that makes this poem *be* what it is *about*.

An oft-quoted example of this use of imagery and structure to create an effect of extreme coalescence between manner of expression and subject of expression which deserves further citation is the passage in which Wordsworth pronounces blessing upon Dorothy's affinity with aspect of weather and landscape, constant symbols in Wordsworth's poetry of creativity and fulfillment. After denying the power of "the dreary intercourse of daily life . . . to prevail against us," Wordsworth raises his hand metaphorically in an attitude very typical of both himself and Coleridge, especially during their years of optimism. What Coleridge does with rhetorical bravado,[23] except perhaps in "Frost at Midnight," Wordsworth does with quiet sincerity:

> Therefore let the moon
> Shine on thee in thy solitary walk;
> And let the misty mountain-winds be free
> To blow against thee: and, in after years,
> When these wild ecstasies shall be matured
> Into a sober pleasure; when thy mind
> Shall be a mansion for all lovely forms,
> Thy memory shall be as a dwelling-place
> For all sweet sounds and harmonies. . . .
>   (ll. 134-142)

Yet, as with all Wordsworth's poetry, it is difficult to show exactly how this passage "works," how to support the declaration that this material *is* what it is *about*. The lines have a self-sufficient clarity that makes quotation essential, and a breath-taking yet simple sincerity that impresses upon the reader not intellectual substance to be ruminated on over a period of time, but the sharp confrontation of a direct experience that Wordsworth has made the reader's. The imagery draws upon associations that are emotional, common in Romantic poetry as we have come to know the tradition, and essentially recreative, rather than descriptive, of experience with art as well as experience with nature. The moon is the beneficent force of exterior creativity. The solitude is the condition essential for confrontation of the self within the creative process. The "misty mountain-winds," another variant of "the correspondent breeze," is especially distinctive and impressive in its combination of wind, rain, and freedom with an intense relationship between two kindred souls.[24] The passage, which through its length builds a unit of experience, making it proper to say that Wordsworth's poetic mind works with grand structures that transform sentences into paragraphs, characterizes these art-nature experiences as "wild ecstasies." These "wild ecstasies" are now put into the perspective of time and change, as if the movement of this passage caught in miniature the movement of the poem as a whole, further strengthening the reader's sense of constantly being in the presence of a structure whose purpose is to create within him the experience the poet is describing in the poem. Again, the language serves a dual theme: the "wild ecstasies," like the "sober pleasures" into which they are to mature, refer not only to the experience of the poet and his sister with nature and with one another, but also to the reader's experience with the poem. As Gérard has pointed out, as readers we have been moving through a number of overlapping cycles in a kind of emotional movement controlled by the poem's structure and imagery which has brought us to a recapitulation of one aspect of the Wordsworthian myth and to a rather complete identification of nature experience with aesthetic experience.[25] The "mansion for all lovely forms" and the "dwelling-place / For all sweet sounds and harmonies" is as much the poem "Tintern Abbey" as it is Dorothy's mind and memory.

Wordsworth's sudden change in focus from the relationship between landscape past and landscape present to the direct address of Dorothy in line 111 embodies the ambiguous and often paradoxical potential of memory as a tool for the evaluation of the quality of life of which Coleridge was well aware:

> We should judge of absent things by the absent. Objects
> which are present are apt to produce perceptions too strong to
> be impartially compared with those recalled only by memory.
> Sir J. Steuart. / (True! and O how often the very opposite is
> true likewise—namely, that the objects of memory are often
> so dear & vivid, that present things are injured by being com-
> pared with them vivid from dearness, &c—)[26]

Wordsworth argues in the concluding section of the poem that as the poem can be an embodiment and transporter of the aesthetic and religious emotions the poet feels in the presence and through his memories of nature, so too another human being of special qualities can serve as surrogate for nature and, like "Tintern Abbey," be a "moveable feast," an embodiment "for all lovely forms . . . for all sweet sounds and harmonies." The terms are purposefully aesthetic and musical. Dorothy shall be the human equivalent of a Wordsworth poem. Of course, Wordsworth's humanization of his poetic impulse and his great affection for his sister had no direct power over the ravages of time, though neither Wordsworth nor his readers could be accused of having such hopes other than in a figurative way.[27] Despite his youthful optimism, Wordsworth obliquely recognizes the potential insufficiency and inferiority of the human vehicle when he adds the phrase "and these my exhortations" to the statement "with what healing thoughts / of tender joy wilt thou remember me, / and these my exhortations" (ll. 144-146), seemingly intent that "these exhortations" refer to the immediate context, his words within the poem. The verbal emphasis of "remember me" expresses Wordsworth's habitual reliance upon oral composition and memory in the writing of his poems.[28] "Lines Composed A Few Miles Above Tintern Abbey," among many other Wordsworth poems, are such "exhortations" in Wordsworth's unique lexicon.

The entire address to Dorothy is suffused with references to poetic communication. It seems no accident that Wordsworth had emphasized earlier that

> *in thy voice I catch*
> *The language of my former heart, and read*
> *My former pleasures in the shooting lights*
> *Of thy wild eyes.*
>
> (ll. 116-119)

This inextricably connects oral and written communication as stages in the creative process, while simultaneously affirming both Dorothy's role as a poem to be read, as if her eyes are a bright page within which are the words of the poem, and the role of the poem as an embodiment of her aesthetic and spiritual qualities. The statement that

> *Nor, perchance—*
> *If I should be no more where I can hear*

> *Thy voice, nor catch from thy wild eyes these gleams*
> *Of past existence—wilt thou then forget*
> *That on the banks of this delightful stream*
> *We stood together. . . .*
>
> (ll. 146-151)

declares "Tintern Abbey" an ever-available recreation of the elevating experience, of the fusion of art and nature, a permanent corrective to forgetfulness. One of the poem's paradoxes is that it proclaims the poem as a victory over the poet's dependence on memory.

It follows rather logically that if "Nature never did betray the heart that loved her," the hearts that love her never will betray their loved one; that minds forged in the image of nature, and humanized by identification with humanity, can themselves be surrogates for nature if the need arises; just as the poem by the complete Wordsworthian poet, who holds the myth in his mind, lives it in his life, and writes his poems about it, can create for the reader a permanent embodiment not only of nature but of the experience of the myth. Though Dorothy falls short of being a poet herself, Wordsworth expands the myth, making its consolations available to non-poets, by promising that what nature has been to him it will be to her also, through the vehicle of his poetry. The psychological level of the myth shall be available to Dorothy, who will move from "solitude, or fear, or pain, or grief" to "tender joy," from depression to exhilaration and consolation, through the permanent availability of revitalizing spots of time in the ideal poetic forms of "Tintern Abbey." The poet has sent out a "kindred mutation" to those who have not literally "stood together" with him; the poem is a mythic account of the life and function of the poet for whom the vehicle of revitalization is nature. "Tintern Abbey" itself is intended to perform a similar function for the reader. Its confidence in man's imagination and the poet's mission distinguishes it as a major achievement of Wordsworth's career and a rare accomplishment in Romantic poetry.

4

Coleridge's Aesthetic Ministry

MOMENTS OF UNDILUTED assurance and affirmation are so rare in Coleridge's career that "Frost at Midnight" (February, 1798), credited as a masterpiece of a new poetic genre,[1] the greater Romantic lyric, and probably a decisive influence on "Tintern Abbey" (July, 1798),[2] stands out as a brief moment of celebration in a chronology of tears. "Frost at Midnight" is a rare achievement: a series of emotions cyclically structured to create a poem whose "fearful symmetry," both awesome and domestic, combines with a series of metaphors to be both example and description of the process of poetic creation. Coleridge was to handle the theme many times in his career,[3] and "Kubla Khan," written about three months later, if Coleridge's memory is accurate,[4] continues the same thematic and

44

structural concern that reached its most subtle but totally non-poetic climax in the *Biographia Literaria* (1817). Like Matthew Arnold fifty years later, Coleridge's concern with the creative process outlasted his poetic creativity. After "Frost at Midnight," he was never again to celebrate his own poetic powers without the qualifications and hesitations visible in "Kubla Khan" and overwhelming in "Dejection: An Ode" (1802).

The quiet beauty of "Frost at Midnight" has evoked quiet appreciation. Humphrey House has remarked that "I think it is much loved; it is certainly much praised; but even so I doubt whether it is adequately appreciated as the perfectly achieved work of art which it is." [5] The most satisfying comments have come from George McLean Harper who emphasized the biographical sweetness of the poem, placing it in a group described by Coleridge's own phrase "Conversation Poems." [6] A much loved poem is sometimes loved to the point of neglect, and House himself began the rectification of this lapse of critical consciousness by emphasizing the importance of the "snake with its Tail in its Mouth," Coleridge's own phrase,[7] the poem whose beginning and ending "perfectly rounds the movement of the mind." [8] Other critics refer to the "return of the poem upon itself" [9] and its "Circular movement," [10] stressing that "the design of such a poem follows and stylizes the dilatory movements of the poet's mind" [11] and that the poem is "a complex, but controlled, statement about the act of cognition." [12] Yet House's remarks are still definitive on the matter of both structure and subject:

> Not only do the movements of the mind give the poem its design and unity; but the poem as a whole leaves us with a quite extraordinary sense of the mind's *very being* in suspense, above time and space; the mind with all its powers of affection and memory, and its power of reading nature as the language of God.[13]

A recent critic's remark that "an important feature of this pattern, and one that is apparent in Coleridge's use of it, is that it makes the whole poem a metaphor of the activity of the poetic sensibility," [14]

carries interpretation still a step further. It is in this direction that
the poem itself takes us; it is essentially a poem whose metaphors,
like its structure, are about the process of creating a poem.[15] Probably for the only time in his career, and with a fullness of sincerity
and commitment that the Romantics only occasionally and the
Victorians hardly ever revealed, Coleridge was able to balance
within a poem all the "miracle[s] of rare device"—the structure of
organicism, the metaphors of art, the subject of poetry, the self as
poet.

When Coleridge originally published "Frost at Midnight" in
Lyrical Ballads (1798), he provided his readers with an explicit
statement about the major metaphors of the poem that he omitted
in the revised version published in 1828 and thereafter. He referred
to

> *the living spirit in our frame,*
> *That loves not to behold a lifeless thing,*
> *Transfuses into all its own delights,*
> *Its own volition, sometimes with deep faith*
> *And sometimes with fantastic playfulness.*

House and others, have claimed that these earlier versions,
"which speak of 'fantastic playfulness' or 'wilful playfulness,'
plainly belong more closely to the insignificant and irresponsible
mood of Cowper," from whose *The Task*, Book IV, "The Winter
Evening," ll. 272-310, Coleridge seems to have gotten the imagery
of the frost and the fire. It is more likely that Coleridge intends in
all seriousness, and as quite consistent with the poem as a whole,
this emphasis upon the capriciousness and the unpredictability of
the poetic imagination.[16] While the phrase "fantastic playfulness"
may have suggested the phrase "curious toys," the phrase "wilful
playfulness" in the next version seems to have suggested the change
to "these wild reliques of our childish Thought," which eventually
became "by its own moods . . . makes a toy of thought." "The living spirit in our frame, / That loves not to behold a lifeless thing"
seems a cognate of the "shaping spirit of imagination" upon which
Coleridge concentrated in "Dejection: An Ode." In "Frost at Mid-

night" the contrast is between, and the analogies are of, the "shaping" frost, the "thin blue flame," the "idling Spirit," the "fluttering stranger," and, finally, "the lovely shapes and sounds intelligible / Of that eternal language," all of which are imagistic variations on both the "deep faith" and the "fantastic playfulness" of the Romantic imagination which insists upon translating all "lifeless things" into "silent icicles," or works of art, through the mediation and transforming power of "the living spirit." Coleridge's revisions testify not to a change in theme, but to an increased confidence in the efficacy of the images to do the job alone.

The poem's dominant image is the frost-icicle relationship, enhanced by the "systolic rhythm" [17] of the poem's structure, both combining to force its end to be its beginning. The revision that omitted the six-line concluding emphasis on the "dear Babe" and simply climaxed with the phrase "quietly shining to the quiet Moon" reveals Coleridge's absolute certainty about the importance of the relationship between the poem's rounded structure and its images. The symmetry of this work of art, this poem, was to be rounded by its major image of creativity. Appropriately, the poem begins with carefully selected external detail in which landscape and natural phenomena are analogies for the topography of the creative spirit and internal psychological conditions: "The Frost performs its secret ministry, / Unhelped by any wind." Some "fantastic," "wilful," playful, powerful yet silent force, seemingly unassisted by any mediative power, any correspondent breeze or obvious reawakening inspiration, transforms a diffuse and unstructured basic element, water, into a substantially and admirably structured new version of that element, icicles. As in Blake's "The Tyger," the "fearful symmetry" is both structural and imagistic, the repetition of the first as the sixth stanza of that poem paralleled by Coleridge's repetition of a variation of his opening in his closing phrase:

> *Or if the secret ministry of frost*
> *Shall hang them up in silent icicles,*
> *Quietly shining to the quiet Moon.*
> (ll. 72-74)

The present tense description of the miraculous creativity of
the frost, whose strange powers suggest some archetype of the
unaided imagination, is followed immediately by a brief past tense
reference to two successive "owlet's" cries. The result is "to toll"
the poet back to his "sole self":

> *The inmates of my cottage, all at rest,*
> *Have left me to that solitude, which suits*
> *Abstruser musings. . . .*
>
> (ll. 4-6)

The contrast is between the permanent creativity of the frost and
the time-contained, time-dominated instance of the poet's self-absorption which indeed, disparaged as "abstruser musings," both in
the context of the poem and of Coleridge's extra-poetic vocabulary, signifies the substitution of thought, of the mind turned in
upon itself, for imagination.[18]

Immediately Coleridge turns to "my cradled infant," the child
who is to play a dominant role in the poem's conclusion and whose
multiple appearances in various transformations does so much to
strengthen our traditional impression of both Coleridge's and
Wordsworth's belief in this Romantic archetype. What often es-
capes notice is their exploitation of the child as a useful device in
the writing of a poem. The utility of the child is that, like landscape, it has both a positive literal presence and maximum symbolic
potential. It can represent many things. Here, Coleridge emphasizes that the child "slumbers peacefully," an image whose contrast
with another representation of the child, done about the same
time, reveals much about the multiple role the child is to play in
"Frost at Midnight":

> The wisdom & graciousness of God in the infancy of the
> human species—its beauty, long continuance &c &c. (Chil-
> dren in the wind—hair floating, tossing, a miniature of the agi-
> tated Trees, below which they play'd—the elder whirling for
> joy, the one in petticoats, a fat Baby, eddying half willingly,
> half by the force of the Gust—driven backward, struggling for-
> ward—both drunk with the pleasure, both shouting their
> hymn of Joy.)

And from the same *Notebooks* section, dated 1797-1798, and headed "Infancy & Infants—":

> *Sports of infants—their incessant activity, the*
> *means being the end.*

> *Kissing itself in the looking-glass.*

> *The Lapland Infant, seeing the sun.*

> *The Souls of Infants, a vision—(vide Swedenborg—)*

> *Some tales of an Infant.*[19]

The infants who are "drunk with pleasure, both shouting their hymn of joy," are figures paralleling Coleridge's projection of himself as Dionysiac poet who "on honey-dew hath fed, / And drunk the milk of Paradise." The "hair floating, tossing" recalls the possessed poet's "flashing eyes" and "floating hair" in "Kubla Khan." The other *Notebooks* selections make clear that Coleridge associated the child with coalescence of being and becoming, means and ends, analogous to his notion that a poem should be what it is about; that the child, like the poet, looks into the mirror of himself, his poem, and finds an image, being both his own and not his own, he can love; that the child, like the poem, has visionary capacities "to see into the heart of things"; and that "tales" or poems are somehow associated with infants, as if the child were a poem and the poem a child. Still other selections from the *Notebooks* make it clear that the child has other meanings and is often associated with a comparatively paternalistic and literal glorification of innocence in a Lockean universe. But Coleridge's association of the infant with the poet, poetry, and the creative process during the period when he wrote "Frost at Midnight" makes the "cradled infant" slumbering "peacefully" a potentially richer figure than has been heretofore considered.

The sleeping child contrasts rather dramatically with the children "drunk with pleasure . . . shouting their hymn of Joy"—inactivity with activity, silence with articulation, somnolent possession with ecstatic abandonment. Yet only the quiet child, Coleridge tells us, saves him from "that solitude, which suits / Abstruser musings." Throughout the poem, Hartley Coleridge's calm presence provides an atmosphere of potential external projection, of possible movement from silence, from "abstruser musings," from the mind turned in upon itself, from negative creativity outwards towards "that eternal language" of which towards the end of the poem he is to become the full representative. The child's seen presence is to become a heard presence (1. 45), as Hartley changes from a symbol of the silent resources of Coleridge's creativity to a symbol of the full expression of his poetic power. Yet, at this point in the poem (ll. 6-7), such transformation has not occurred. It is only hinted in the common silence that ties together the frost and the child; the external force of unaided creativity observed awesomely by the poet only through a barrier and the potential ecstasy of the slumbering child. Of course, none of these phenomena are yet definitely affirmative. The power of the frost outside almost mocks the impotence of the power inside the poet, and the transformation of the child exists only in potential. There is another danger sign. Both the frost and the child reinforce the silence and the solitude which are characteristics of a possibly dangerous atmosphere for Coleridge in which "abstruse researchers" may replace imagination.

Though there is nothing arguable in the conclusion that "a recurrent theme of the conversation poems is that the sounds and sights of nature combine to teach us of the changing separateness, yet constant oneness, of life," [20] it is not here that Coleridge puts the emphasis in "Frost at Midnight," which is more about poetic creativity and the poet than about natural creativity and nature. The extreme silence and solitude of the poem's opening, punctuated by a noise emphasizing the silence and by a presence which has only possible ecstasy, is a negative environment and the frost an awesome and certainly inhuman force, some unreachable prototype of a creativity unavailable to the poet. Keats's nightingale has a similar function, though the elusiveness of the bird increases as the poem develops, whereas ultimately Coleridge is to find solace and reconciliation in the notion that the slumbering child will someday become the master of the marriage of oppositions, of frost and fire reconciled and the individual human spirit in harmony and at peace with itself. The unnatural silence, the existence of articulation only in potential, seems to undermine any possibilities of articulation at all:

> *'Tis calm indeed! so calm, that it disturbs*
> *And vexes meditation with its strange*
> *And extreme silentness. Sea, hill, and wood,*
> *This populous village! Sea, and hill, and wood,*
> *With all the numberless goings-on of life,*
> *Inaudible as dreams!*
>
> (ll. 8-13)

This inaudibility of normally audible phenomena implies the ambiguity of the "secret Frost," suggesting both the latent constructive and destructive characteristics of the creative process that in its negative form, a storm gone out of control, dominates Coleridge's consideration of the same subject in "Dejection: An Ode." In "Frost at Midnight," there is no howling storm, no destructive wind, neither is there a reawakening correspondent breeze, nor indeed any wind *at all* in the opening of the poem. Yet the conclusion not only notes the infant's "gentle breathing," but speculates on Hartley who will "wander like a breeze." The preternatural, foreboding silence is to be transformed into a vision of the highest poetic articulation, "the lovely shapes and sounds intelligible / Of that eternal language. . . ."

The image of silence is followed immediately by an image of devitalization and exhaustion, "the thin blue flame / Lies on my low-burnt fire, and quivers not" (ll. 13-14), suggesting that the consumption of literal fuel should be extended to imply a depletion of spiritual and creative fuel.[21] It is hard to imagine that Coleridge would not have felt and been aware of the obvious psychological and symbolic extension of this image. Significantly, the basic physical materials of the major images of the opening section of the poem, frost and fire, are identical with the major image of the paradoxical nature of the work of art in "Kubla Khan," "that sunny dome! those caves of ice!" The correspondence is made more specific by the lines Coleridge omitted from later versions of the poem. Originally, at this point in "Frost at Midnight," Coleridge conceived of the fire on the grate as both expression and catalyst of his creative powers, emphasizing that

> *the living spirit in our frame,*
> *That loves not to behold a lifeless thing,*
> *Transfuses into all its own delights. . . .*

Yet the confusion and the inappropriateness of the expression seem to have been evident to Coleridge and probably account for his omission of these lines from later editions. The context of the image will not permit a reconciliation between fire and ice. It calls for exhaustion, not vitalization, fragmentation, not unity. The "thin blue flame" too clearly suggests the lowness of the poet's spirit and creativity to represent also what the "living spirit" can transform into a brighter flame. Of course, the transformation of emptiness into creativity, through the vehicle of the child rather than the fire, of silence into sound, must come at the climax, not at the beginning, of the poem.

The fascinating manner in which Coleridge postpones and coalesces images in the service not only of his theme but of the dramatic structure of his poem is clear from the revisions of the poem's first part and from the omission in later versions of the six lines with which the poem concluded in 1798. Again, the justification of the revision has much less to do with what House claims would be the "increasing shapelessness" of the poem "once the vista of new domestic detail was opened" than with Coleridge's craftsmanlike desire to reconcile, as he does less affirmatively in "Kubla Khan," the images of fire and water which he has presented in the first section and then neglected.[22] The point is one of emphasis: immediately prior to the concluding lines which return to the "secret ministry of frost" of the opening lines, Coleridge synthesizes or coalesces the two previously unreconcilable images, the dim internal fire and the mysterious external frost. The redbreast may

> *sit and sing*
> *Betwixt the tufts of snow on the bare branch*
> *Of mossy apple-tree, while the nigh thatch*
> *Smokes in the sun-thaw. . . .*
>
> (ll. 67-70)

The snow-ice and the sun-thaw shall be the backdrop of natural but miraculous transformation against which the bird shall sing. Again, the revisions of the poem are more central than previous commentators have thought.

All versions, however, emphasize the association early in the poem (ll. 15-20) of the fire with sound, "the sole unquiet thing," suggesting that it too, like the slumbering child, has the potential for extension, for expansion into vitality, ecstasy, and joy, and for the association of the dim flame on the grate with the poet himself, whose fire is not quite extinguished and who certainly is attempting to extend himself:

> *Methinks, its motion in this hush of nature*
> *Gives it dim sympathies with me who live,*
> *Making it a companionable form. . . .*
>
> (ll. 17-19)

The poet and the flame share frustration, self-torment, and devitalization:

> *Whose puny flaps and freaks the idling Spirit*
> *By its own moods interprets, every where*
> *Echo or mirror seeking of itself,*
> *And makes a toy of Thought.*
>
> (ll. 20-23)

Because he insists, Coleridge tells us, on imposing mind on matter, artificiality on naturalness, "abstruse researches" on creative imagination, he cannot do otherwise than conclude that the dim fire is a symbol of his own shrunkenness, while at the same time recognizing that his epistemology and its expression are destructive.[23]

While Coleridge here has escaped the "depression too dreadful to be described," [24] which he not so easily evaded "in after years," he has done so through a moment of stasis, a pause in time, in thought, even in breathing, permitting him to hold in abeyance the possible conflict between frost and fire, child and adult, silence and articulation, impotence and creativity. This has been done through a series of half-stated equations in which each factor on both sides of the equation has a dual, sometimes ambiguous, existence, both a positive and a negative charge to its element, making the balance even more delicate. The poem seems almost to hold its breath, moving like a graceful sleepwalker between dangers of which it seems both conscious and unconscious, always in a moment of silent pause between potentially conflicting realities. The inaudibility, the absence of quivering, the extreme silence, the hush of nature, all suggest Coleridge's strategy of escape from depression. Emotional responsiveness is to be minimized, as if the feelings were in deep freeze, metabolism and the pulse of life slowed down, the vital spirit of creativity reduced to a "thin blue flame . . . on my low-burnt fire." Coleridge's poetry often seems the intensely hot product of molten emotions; yet in "Frost at Midnight" he has "cooled it" in a way that creates a mood of control, calmness, and certitude that he can hardly match again. Certainly Wordsworth must have had this example in mind when six months later in "Tintern Abbey" he created his lengthy "oh! how oft" sequence (ll. 50-57) in the very rhetoric as well as with the sentiment that Coleridge expressed in lines 23-26 of "Frost at Midnight":

> But O! how oft,
> How oft, at school, with most believing mind,
> Presageful, have I gazed upon the bars,
> To watch that fluttering stranger! and as oft. . . .

Like Wordsworth, Coleridge turns to the past for an explanation of the present. Whereas for the former the symbol of positive and pleasurable continuity is the river Wye, for Coleridge the exterior landscape is not nearly as meaningful a source for poetic and personal symbols as are the elements frost and fire. The latter are more direct, more easily internalized, less encumbered with the reality of particular place and particular time. Coleridge has a less literal and more visionary imagination than does Wordsworth, often leaping from internal states to an allegorical or visionary external landscape or image to express his feelings. Thus, the "stranger" that Coleridge gazes upon is a multiple version of himself and his poetry. The assumption that "these films are called strangers and are supposed to portend the arrival of some absent friend" reinforces the continuity between the infertility of the present and similar moods of the past.[25] The flame is both the low ebb of the creative spirit which has not yet gone out and the expectation of the increase of that flame. It is the potential arrival of some absent friend, of some new impulse towards and product of artistic creativity, that Coleridge wants by sympathetic attraction not only to connect past and present but to revivify the present. Coleridge is recreating in his memory a past experience extraordinarily similar to one in the present, which is described in the first section of the poem. The second section of the poem, then, is another version of the initial experience.

In the second section, the film on the grate promises the boy that the stranger will come. Yet experience, in the form of "the stern preceptor," undermines the certainty, reducing it to a hope with which the section concludes: "For still I hoped to see the *stranger's* face. . . ." Between the experience described in section two and that described in section one, the shadow has fallen. Incertitude has become dominant, so that the noticeable characteristic of the poet as he describes himself in the present is his complete absence of faith in the fulfillment of the prophecy. The stranger is not even mentioned in the first section of "Frost at Midnight" which concludes with an irritated complaint in which the flickering and dream-like quality of the fire on the grate is compared to the self-involved egocentricity of the poet's mind turned in upon itself. Whereas in the first section "all the numberless goings-on of life" are as "inaudible as dreams," in the second, the dream-like world is the poet's interior one in which dreams are sweet, innocent, and richly pleasureable. Formerly, gazing at the film on the grate did not suggest the relationship between the "thin blue flame" and the thin life of the poet or the parallel between its negative self-involvement and his own. As often as he stared at the film

> as oft
> With unclosed lids, already had I dreamt
> Of my sweet birth-place, and the old church tower. . . .
>   (ll. 26-28)

Instead of tolling him back to his "sole self," the bells from the church tower, providing the audible accompaniment in section two that the "owlet's cry" supplies in section one,

> stirred and haunted me
> With a wild pleasure, falling on mine ear
> Most like articulate sounds of things to come!
>   (ll. 31-33)

Certainly these sounds are "presageful" of "the lovely shapes and sounds intelligible / Of that eternal language" which, in the third section, climax Coleridge's vision of what the creativity of his son will accomplish and which, at the same time, represent his own poetic aspirations, his own aesthetic ministry, whose message he embodies in this poem, representing what "Frost at Midnight" is intended to be. He brooded, then, on the possibilities of language, of his future poetic art, when all versions of the absent friend, the sought-after companion and completion, were to be coalesced into the reality of a unified and fulfilled maturity. In "Frost at Midnight," Coleridge comes as close to that unity and fulfillment as he ever was to come. Those sound-induced, open-lidded dreams of the past produced sleep in which those dreams were prolonged until jarred by "the stern preceptor's face," which the boy attempts to deceive:

> *Fixed with mock study on my swimming book:*
> *Save if the door half opened, and I snatched*
> *A hasty glance, and still my heart leaped up,*
> *For still I hoped to see the stranger's face. . . .*
>   (ll. 38-41)

It is almost a prescient summary of Coleridge's career in which "false study" and the spontaneous search for "the stranger's face" uneasily coexisted in the heart and mind of an intensely lonely man.

In the return of the third section to the first, there is a return to the sleeping child in a developed if not transformed version. Whereas previously he had been subordinated to the silence and the mocking infertility of "the idling Spirit," he now becomes an articulate embodiment of life whose audible presence, "whose gentle breathings,"

> *Fill up the interspersèd vacancies*
> *And momentary pauses of the thought!*
>   (ll. 46-47)

Silence gives way to organized and regular sound which turns the poet's attention away from vacancies that vex, from non-productive self-absorption, so that the infant's breathing is both the formal structuring element and the element that is being structured in the transformed present. The child's breathing is like music, an emphasis on articulation that Coleridge uses throughout the poem to exploit the non-literary nature of music which demands that form and substance be identical.[26] Frost and fire are appropriate accompanying images. These are elements whose coalescence of structure and substance make them "miracles of rare device," suggesting that both the formal structure and the substantive images of the poem attempt to achieve a coalescence permitting "Frost at Midnight" to be what it is about, a poem about poetry. Its major effect on the reader will be to produce an aesthetic response while communicating this poet's particular version of what he himself is as poet and how he believes the poetic process works. It is a kind of lesson through example.

If frost and fire are images of creativity, the "dear Babe" of the third stanza, consequently, is not only that but a symbol of the work of art itself. Significantly, it is at this point in the poem that the child is described as possessing the visionary characteristics it so noticeably lacked in its "slumbering" in the first section. Though, indeed, obvious that as image the child is Coleridge's to do with as he pleases, the difference is not in the child itself but in Coleridge who moves from the vexed sterility of the first section to a renewal of feeling in the third, using the child as a vehicle rather than as an absolute. For the reader, the child becomes a representative of the poem and of poetry. Just as Coleridge exclaims,

> My babe so beautiful! it thrills my heart
> With tender gladness, thus to look at thee,
> (ll. 48-49)

so too the reader by force of influence must exclaim on the beauties of what the child represents, of what it too thrills "to look at." This child has been transformed into one whose "means" is his "end," who is "seeing the sun," who himself is "a vision," and tells "tales of an infant," and, most importantly, is potentially "drunk with pleasure," shouting his "hymn of Joy." To prepare us for this transformation and to emphasize both how close yet how distant he as poet is to this child, Coleridge proclaims the contrast between his own youth and the youth Hartley will have. This child, "this stranger" who has finally come, is both part of yet separate from him. The impulse of partial renunciation is one that runs through Coleridge's life. He constantly attempts to find stratagems to compensate for what he deeply feels as losses. He connects himself directly or indirectly to those whom he believes have not experienced the same loss or are at least closer to those things or states of feeling that he is convinced he no longer possesses. The ultimate deprivation is to be the loss of his creative ability, his imaginative responses as well as his disciplined handling of language within poetic structures. Even as early as 13 December 1796, he was good-humoredly and with "presageful" rationalization anticipating the adjustment to loss:

> But Literature, tho' I shall never abandon it, will always be a secondary object with me— My poetic Vanity & my political Furore have been exhaled; And I would rather be an expert, self-maintaining Gardener than a Milton, if I could not unite both.[27]

The reference to a "self-maintaining gardener" ironically suggests the originality and independence of Coleridge as critic, but I suspect that Coleridge hardly meant it that way in 1796. Of course, he could not unite both. However, Coleridge proclaims that the child will:

>   *wander like a breeze*
> *By lakes and sandy shores, beneath the crags*
> *Of ancient mountain. . . .*
> . . . .
>   *so [will he] see and hear*
> *The lovely shapes and sounds intelligible*
> *Of that eternal language, which [his] God*
> *Utters, who from eternity doth teach*
> *Himself in all, and all things in himself.*
> *Great universal Teacher! he shall mould*
> *[his] spirit, and by giving make it ask.*
>   (ll. 54-64)

For Coleridge and for others, the child as poet and poem shall be both inspiration and inspired, whose substance will embody the truths that are inherent in aspects of the natural world, coalescing both sight and sound into a special language whose major characteristic shall be its visual prominence and its aural distinctiveness. The child will have the visionary and ecstatic experience of identification with God as archetypal poet and with the poem, "the lovely shapes and sounds intelligible / Of that eternal language," as the vehicle of God's communication with man. No wonder, then, that not only "all seasons shall be sweet to thee," as the final section states, but that the poet's achievement shall be the coalescence of fire and water in a general series of recurrent transformations that proclaim the ultimate unity of all things. The image is one of liquidity in which there are "tufts of snow," "the nigh thatch" that "smokes in the sun-thaw," the fall of the "eave-drops," and, of course, "the secret ministry of frost." All these are states in the creative process and images of the poem.

They are images that Coleridge was not able to reconcile as calmly and as confidently ever again. The renewal of emotion and confidence in creativity through the vehicle of the child, the working out of the problem in an isolated moment of silence, gives way to the loud and destructive blast of the "Mad Lutinist," the storm of "Dejection: An Ode," whose conclusion hardly persuades us that it brings real relief from the "stifled, drowsy, unimpassioned grief." Whereas in "Frost at Midnight" Coleridge affirms that this liquidity, this continual transforming power of creativity, represented by the alternatives of water dripping in the wind, "whether the eave-drops fall / Heard only in the trances of the blast," and water turning to ice in the frost, can flourish both in sound and in silence, just as the poem moves from silence to sound, from ice to fire, and combines them both, in "Dejection" the "blast" is explicitly destructive. Even when the storm is over, the other "tale" it tells "of a little child / Upon a lonesome wild" who "moans low in bitter grief and fear" radically transforms and denies the potential "hymn of joy" of the infant of "Frost at Midnight." Though the blessing with which "Dejection" concludes has a similarity with the charismatic prayers with which "Tintern Abbey" and "Frost at Midnight" end, Coleridge's explicit exclusion of himself in the latter poem from the creative fulfillment that he envisions for Hartley takes on a more tragic tone in a work in which there is no successful vehicle of release and renewal.

In the year of his greatest productivity as poet, Coleridge wrote that "I find true Joy after a sincere prayer; but for want of habit my mind wanders, and I cannot pray as I ought." [28] The wandering of his mind became the beginning of a poem of affirmation, and prayer for others became a standard gesture of his greatest poetry, so deeply does it seem that Coleridge was aware of and magnified his own deficiencies.[29] In his poetry he cannot pray for himself.

Whether or not "Coleridge was led from poetry to love to "abstruse researches," in his quest for salvation," [30] a fiercely pursued controversy, certainly one recent critic is correct when he observes that "the creation of poetry" forced Coleridge "to look deep into himself in a self-contemplation that became finally too painful to bear because it contradicted all he wanted to believe about himself and his universe." [31] Frost, fire, silence, sound, wind, child, and prayer are the images that best characterize the aesthetic nature of a ministry which reached its minor peak of affirmation in "Frost at Midnight" and its major desert of denial in "Dejection: An Ode." Coleridge's collapse into insecurity about his function as poet and the value of poetry marks a major stage in the development of Romantic and Victorian self-consciousness. Anxiety is almost too mild a word to express the depth of Coleridge's fears and self-doubts. Empedocles' plunge into the volcano and Arnold's rejection of "Empedocles on Etna" because of its stifling and self-tormenting inwardness are later stages of the development in nineteenth-century poetry epitomized by Coleridge's "Dejection: An Ode" and his gradual relinquishment of his role as poet for the role of literary and cultural analyst.

5

The Architecture of "Locksley Hall"

"LOCKSLEY HALL" IS a poem caught between the Romantic meditative ode and the dramatic monolog. It anticipates the Victorian objectification into narrative poetry of the major themes expressed by the Romantics in lyric forms. Critics have argued that its flaw is one of dramatic credibility, the limited independence of the narrator.[1] Tennyson could not decide decisively whether the speaker was to be a thinly disguised version of the poet himself or an independent fictional character in a dramatic monolog. He is something of both, though more of the former. Consequently, the poem has greater affinity with the Romantic meditative ode, a tradition that Tennyson knew very well, than with the masks and disguises of the Victorian dramatic monolog or with the objective narrative that

Tennyson was to employ so successfully on the same themes in "Merlin and Vivien." While "Locksley Hall" looks forward to the dominance of the dramatic monolog, its basic affiliation is with poems like "Ode to a Nightingale" and "Dejection: An Ode." Certainly no one can argue the weakness of these poems on the grounds of genre. As "Tintern Abbey" is a Romantic meditative ode or greater Romantic lyric in everything but meter, versification, and stanzaic form, so too is "Locksley Hall." It is structured basically as a record of psychological or emotional movement in which the poem's structure is the poem's theme, the movement from the poet's doubts concerning his creativity and commitment towards affirmation of his "ministry." The great storm with which the poem concludes may be more Coleridgean than Carlylean, more in the tradition of the "correspondent breeze" than in the tradition of

> *On, to the bound of the waste,*
> *On, to the City of God.*

The major affirmation of the poem is the affirmation of the creative spirit:

> *O, I see the crescent promise of my spirit*
> *hath not set.*
> *Ancient founts of inspiration well thro'*
> *all my fancy yet.*[2]

Like "Tintern Abbey," Tennyson's poem attempts to understand and explain the present through an exploration of the past. The speaker is melancholy, despondent. The "dreary gleams about the moorland" are representative of a present that has been made impotent by the past, the darkness and loss of vitality symbolized by Locksley Hall. The doleful "early morn" of the present and its harsh realities are compared to the brilliantly clear star-bright nights of the past:

> *Many a night from yonder ivied casement, ere*
> *I went to rest,*

> *Did I look on great Orion sloping slowly to the west.*
> (ll. 7-8)

Parodoxically, the moments before that sleep were ones of hope, for in that sleep such dreams did come while now, in the present, the morning is the time of sober confrontation of the actual.[3]

Immediately, one of the major dreams, the vision of humanitarian progress, is presented. But Tennyson the poet quickly turns from the temptation of this abstraction; the possibility of an intense and enduring love was connected in the past to his sense of poetic destiny. The succeeding stanzas emphasize a motif that is to be elaborated later in the poem, the importance of the primacy of the feelings, of the unrestrained expression of one's deepest self. Ironically, the cramping or the restraint of feelings may lead to the full expression of them, just as this review of the past is to lead to a fuller understanding and expression of the needs of the present. As in the tradition of the Romantic meditative ode, feelings are the keys to reality:

> *'They were dangerous guides the feelings—*
> *she herself was not exempt—*
> *Truly, she herself had suffer'd'— Perish in*
> *thy self-contempt!*
> (ll. 95-96)

All that the heart feels is true.

In the next ten stanzas, the promise of love is balanced by the treason of love. The ideals of the wedded bliss of the poet and his wife are contrasted with the sordid reality of the ideal, mated not with the noble poet but with the base and unfeeling bourgeois.[4] Amy is not a real woman; the man she has married is not a real man. The rhetoric that Tennyson uses to describe his outrage, often described as shrill and petulant,[5] has some justification if Amy represents the ultimate completion of the poet's self. Without her, he is less poet, if poet at all. Without her, his creative imagination, lacking the essential complement of love, turns sterile. Amy's husband, then, represents not simply philistine bestiality but some principle of reality that stands between the poet and his own self-completion. Of course, he represents also Carlyle's materialistic philistine and is the image of Tennyson's detestation of the dominance of bearish values, of the general triumph of vulgarity and economics over sentiment:

> *Cursed be the sickly forms that err from honest*
> *   Nature's rule!*
> *Cursed be the gold that gilds the straiten'd*
> *   forehead of the fool!*
>
> (ll. 61-62)

But "Locksley Hall" is a poem about Tennyson, not about Victorian culture. The detailed description of the bestiality of Amy's relationship with her husband avoids both boorishness and irrelevance because Tennyson convinces us that the bitterness is his own, a product of a worthy theme, the treason which prevents the fulfillment of his spiritual and poetic self. As for Coleridge and Keats, the treason ultimately is self-treason, some failure of confidence within the poet about the efficacy of his creative powers and the value of his poetic achievement. In a sense, Amy would have been created if she had not existed, as Andrea del Sarto creates Lucrezia as the outward symbol of his own inner loss of vital power, as Merlin creates Vivien to represent the dark and self-destructive aspect of his own melancholy personality.

Tennyson's general optimism comes partially from his belief that this betrayal of ideals is not inherent in the nature of things, that his temporary non-completion of his poetic self results from environmental rather than from organic causes. The perversion and depravation of the ideal derives from "social wants" and "social lies." For "the sickly forms . . . err from honest Nature's rule." As for Wordsworth, for Tennyson there is a moral norm built into the world order. The "sickly forms" refer to man's grotesque distortions of these rules, while at the same time suggesting both the gross physical bestiality of Amy's husband and the psychological weakness that taints her lithe figure. Tennyson refers to his tone as "bluster": "Well—'tis well that I should bluster!— / Hadst thou less unworthy proved," signaling that the unrestrained emotional resentment of this long section of the poem has been part of the strategy of examining the past in order to change the present. Now he can put into perspective the personal elements of this affair and turn the trite story into a Victorian version of the failed ideal, the poet's exorcism of the failure and the impotence that it has produced. Certainly the "high-born maiden" archetype is there, but mainly as one element in the larger Romantic notion of the tension between reality and ideal in the context of the poet's concern for his own creativity.[6]

The change in tone signals the return to the same imagery but on a different level. Lines 63-96 retrace the same route as lines 39-58. Whereas the invective of the earlier section took the form of emotionally outraged images of bestiality, the latter section calmly dismisses the worthiness of Amy to function as the poet's anima, his poetic other half, union with whom might produce perfect creativity. The emotion becomes one recollected in tranquility, through the prism of a higher perspective. The disappointment of the failed ideal is seen as an experience and an emotion necessary to the new direction in which the poet is moving: "This is truth the poet sings, / That a sorrow's crown of sorrow is remembering happier things" (ll. 75-76). The "sorrow's crown," in its ambiguity, suggests both sorrow as intense pain and the royal crown the poet wears, symbol of the deep feelings and personal experience on which his poetry is based.

Tennyson writes:

> Like a dog, he hunts in dreams, and thou art
>   staring at the wall,
> Where the dying night-lamp flickers, and the
>   shadows rise and fall,
>
> (ll. 79-80)

contrasting this barren nighttime with the "many a night [he] saw the Pleiads," earlier in the poem, the poet's youthful dream of brilliant night contrasted with Amy's permanent loss of the "gleam" as represented by Tennyson himself. The images of conjugal unhappiness are counterbalanced by those of maternal satisfaction. Amy's symbolic role in the growth, development, and completion of the poet is concluded when she becomes a representation of the death of the feelings, a complete renunciation of her role as the poet's other half. Appropriately, this section of the poem concludes with the projection of Amy as a representative of the enemies of creativity:

> *With a little hoard of maxims preaching down*
> > *a daughter's heart.*
> *'They were dangerous guides the feelings—she*
> > *herself was not exempt. . . .'*
>
> > > > (ll. 94-95)

The poet's recovery and salvation ultimately are to come from mixing "with action, lest [he] wither[s] by despair."

The structural center of the poem (ll. 97-144) contains the key to the nature of that glorified "action" as well as the major contrast between the poet of the present, the poet of "sad experience," and the comparatively unsophisticated poet of youthful visions. The poet asks:

> *What is that which I should turn to, lighting upon*
> > *days like these?*
> *Every door is barr'd with gold, and opens but to*
> > *golden keys.*
>
> > > > (ll. 99-100)

His search is for a field of action, yet the great emphasis placed upon the limitation of action by a materialistic society is somewhat misleading. The essential contrast is not between materialistic society at large and the general spiritual values of the speaker, though certainly this antinomy accurately assumes that the poet has rejected the possibility that he desires to grasp the "golden keys" and enter that "door" or "gate." Rather, the true contrast is between the "angry fancy," expressed quite vividly in the earlier section of the poem where Tennyson berates the treason of Amy and the bestiality of her new life, and the need to harness that "angry fancy" within poetic action, "the act of the mind," that will fulfill the poet's sense of his heroic destiny as poet. The question is: "I have but an angry fancy; what is that which I should do?" The immediate answer is to relive the past through memory and meditation; the long-range answer is found in the "rain or hail, or fire or snow."

But images from nature, as they are for Wordsworth in "Tintern Abbey," cannot be sufficient vehicles of revitalization for Tennyson. Marshall McLuhan says that "it is, perhaps, a mistake to regard nature as the subject-matter of the Romantics. They wanted not just to see it but to see through it; and failing that they made it an objective correlative for states of mind that are independent of it." [7] Only Wordsworth among the Romantics succeeded in this difficult triumph, in full commitment to his myth of nature as an image for poetry. Blake and Byron really would have none of it, though for radically different reasons of philosophy and temperament. Keats and Shelley, in their mature phases, went in other directions. And Coleridge was perhaps the first to reject the ideal Wordsworthian balance between nature and the imagination. By the mid-1830's, nature had been demythologized enough to make it untenable as a symbol or vehicle in a process of the rebirth of the poetic imagination, though its degradation is not completely evident until close to the mid-century, in poems like Arnold's "To Marguerite" and "Empedocles on Etna." [8] In "Locksley Hall," Tennyson seems to be aware of this, for he does not fail for want of trying other vehicles: the first of which is the return to the past through memory; the second, the flight to some paradise of idealized Romantic experience; the third, a vivid embrace of the Christian European commitment in terms of the individual poet and the tradition, "the ancient founts of inspiration."

The return to the past is an attempt to revivify creative energy, to

> Make me feel the wild pulsation that I felt
>   before the strife,
> When I heard my days before me, and the tumult
>   of my life . . .
>
> (ll. 109-110)

The utopian vision of the succeeding lines is presented as a possible ideal context for the proper "action" of the poet.[9] Whereas in that special "tumult" of "Kubla Khan," which comes from the merging of the river into the "lifeless sea," "Kubla heard from far / Ancestral voices prophesying war," in Tennyson's "tumult" of personal energy and hope he has had a great vision of universal peace and progress. But both secular European utopia and primitive Polynesian utopia are to prove equally unfertile fields of action for the poet. The emphasis is upon personal feeling recaptured by memory—"wild pulsation," "tumult," "large excitement," "eager-hearted," "spirit leaps." This vigorous potentiality of the past is to be contrasted with the sad enervation of the present in the poem's opening. Characteristically, Tennyson makes use of a traditional image of the English imagination to convey the sense of excitement and the potential for the fulfillment of creative and ambitions:

> *Yearning for the large excitement that the*
> *coming years would yield,*
> *Eager-hearted as a boy when first he leaves*
> *his father's field,*
> *And at night along the dusky highway near and*
> *nearer drawn,*
> *Sees in heaven the light of London flaring*
> *like a dreary dawn.*
>
> (ll. 111-114)

The historical urban magnet of English life draws the hopeful young poet towards his destiny and its variety, as Paul Morel, in the final passages of *Sons and Lovers*, is to gaze at the lights of London in the distance, symbolizing his liberation and his new life. Yet this London is represented also as a "dreary dawn," recalling the "dreary gleams about the moorland" of the poem's opening lines and perhaps suggesting the ultimate Tennysonian rejection of the cosmopolitan European city as an appropriate field of action for the poet. London is connected to the young poet's failed vision of man's secular perfectability. To complete the metaphor Tennyson describes his youthful alter ago whose "spirit leaps within him to be gone before him then, / Underneath the light he looks at, in among the throngs of men" (ll. 115-116), descending beneath that artificial "dreary dawn" of city lights into the city of utopian brotherhood and scientific wonder that is to prove just as unviable as the Camelot of *Idylls of the King.*

In this paradise "the kindly earth shall slumber, lapt in universal law" in consonance with "honest Nature's rules." "So I triumphed," Tennyson writes, "ere my passion sweeping thro' me left me dry," suggesting that the victory in the past was prelapsarian and unsophisticated. Confrontation with experience, the reality of Amy's treason, proves the triumph to have been too easily attained, unearned and therefore unenduring. Appropriately, then, Tennyson concludes this section with a description of the *acidia* of his spirit in the tradition of Keats's "drowsy numbness," the sickness unto death that the crucified king represents in Browning's "Saul." The degree of pastness here is important, for the "triumph" has been followed by defeat, which in turn has been followed by explanation for the failure of this future to materialize. The slow pace of science, the demands of urban democracy, the emphasis upon material progress, the diminution of the Christian vision of spiritual perfection, the increased centralization and power of the state, the gap between man's power and his ability to use that power wisely, all these are elements in the failure of utopianism, secular or religious, to provide the poet with a settled frame and an eager mind. Despite the poet's personal belief in a purposeful universe and the gradual, long-range expansion of man's spirituality:

> Yet I doubt not thro' the ages one increasing
>   purpose runs,
> And the thoughts of men are widen'd with the
>   process of the suns,
>
> (ll. 137-138)

his current mood can only be one of depression and failure:

> *What is that to him that reaps not harvest of*
>   *his youthful joys,*
> *Tho' the deep heart of existence beat forever*
>   *like a boy's?*
>
> (ll. 139-140)

He has not found completion. Consequently he has not found the powers of fullest expression, either in his attempt to merge with a spiritual ideal or in his vision of brotherhood and scientific progress.

History, Tennyson suggests, can be dismissed as a set of illusions which time destroys, and the only solid foundation for personal optimism is in personal achievement. Appropriately, then, the melancholy of the opening, followed by the two-part account of the treason of Amy, separated by a condemnation of the "social wants," the first shrill and bitter, the second resigned and philosophical, is climaxed by major emphasis on the problem of the renewal of the feelings and the need of the poet to channel his creative energies. An attempt to reawaken the energy of the past is followed by an analysis of the gap between youthful visions of progress and actual retrogression or, at best, slow movement forward. The comparatively sophisticated poet, in the present again, having exorcized the past and some of the enervation it has produced, champions the stoic philosophy of the poet who "bears a laden breast, / Full of sad experience, moving towards the stillness of his rest" (ll. 143-144).

The final sections present the second and third possibilities for symbolic vehicles, which will bring coherency to the poet and the poem, and conclude with a prayerful invocation in the tradition of the Romantic meditative ode. The penultimate section begins with a literal return to the active present of the poem. The bugle horn sounds in the distance, and Tennyson, provoked by his knowledge that the world of non-poets scorns his "foolish passion," describes woman in the traditional Miltonic sense as "the lesser man" and proclaims his liberation from the need for unity with some actual woman, representative of his completion as poet or not. Just as Andrea del Sarto takes as an emblem of his dependence his need for

Lucrezia, and as emblem of his great contemporaries' independence their absence of wives, so too Tennyson now rejects dependence upon an outer anima for completion. Man the poet can be a
self-sustaining creature on the imaginative level, for

> *Woman is the lesser man, and all thy passions,*
>   *match'd with mine,*
> *Are as moonlight unto sunlight, and as water*
>   *unto wine.*
>
> (ll. 151-152)

The tone has changed decisively. Whereas earlier, in order to
put the present into perspective, Tennyson had explored the failures of the past, using the traditional themes of the female betrayer
and the science fiction future, now with a sudden burst of hopeful
emotion, as if liberated by his rejection of dependency, he uses the
noble savage to represent the dream of the great escape from dec-
adent European society. His imagery is marvelously synthetic and
revealing. He introduces us to the notion that the speaker is an orphan whose "evil-starred" father died in battle in India, an instance
of the tendency in nineteenth-century English literature to symbol-
ize alienation and psychological isolation as a state of orphanhood,
which Dickens, for example, does so frequently. At the same time,
the India motif, land of mystery and wealth, of death for the many
and riches for the few, anticipates, with its imperialistic overtones,
the symbolic embracing of the European Christian commitment
and the rejection of the "gray barbarian." Naturally, the orphan is
left "a selfish uncle's ward." The poet now dreams of bypassing the
uncle, England, and all of Europe to return to his true father, his
ultimate origin, "deep in yonder shining Orient, where [his] life
began to beat." As in most Romantic poetry, the true father is a
symbolic father, often replaced or usurped by a false father, and
the poet's search is for the source of his own lost creativity.

In lines 157-172, Tennyson presents his version of the ultimately unsatisfactory paradise in which, as in Wordsworth's "The
Tables Turned," the world of books and vicarious experience is rejected for direct action of the most instinctive and passionate sort.

This limited version of the epistemological utopia of the Romantic imagination in which all learning is a continuous state of total exposure to a favorable environment is transformed in Tennyson's imagination into a sensual Eden, associated in his other poems with extreme eroticism and death. The sensuality of the verse and the theme have much in common with stanzas V and VI of "Ode to a Nightingale," and indeed Tennyson does dismiss his vision with the implicit admission that "for many a time / I have been half in love with easeful Death." The obvious comparison is between European activity and Oriental or Polynesian quietude, immersement in time contrasted with absorption into eternity. Yet the lines that immediately follow emphasize a variant, if not a contradiction, of this contrast, indicating that the theme of the renewal of feeling and creativity stressed earlier is a consistent, perhaps dominant, concern of the poem as a whole:

> *There the passions cramp'd no longer shall have*
> *scope and breathing space;*
> *I will take some savage woman, she shall rear*
> *my dusky race.*
> *Iron-jointed, supple-sinew'd, they shall dive,*
> *and they shall run,*
> *Catch the wild goat by the hair, and hurl their*
> *lances in the sun;*
> *Whistle back the parrot's call, and leap the*
> *rainbows of the brooks,*
> *Not with blinded eyesight poring over miserable*
> *books.*
>
> (ll. 167-172)

This Oriental paradise is depicted as a place of action, not as a retreat into blissful nirvana. The action involves a full, free expression of "the passions." Tennyson here refers both to sexuality and to the "feelings." The products of these "[un]cramp'd" expressions are explicitly a new "dusky race" and implicitly the Romantic creations of the liberated poet. Tennyson has drawn upon the theme of the noble savage and his new-found land, even including marriage, sacred subject in Tennyson's poetry and life, with "some savage woman," as a metaphor to express the urge towards free and confident creativity. That he could use this metaphor, even in a pattern that rejects its substance, is great tribute both to the flexibility of his imagination and to the strong hold of this metaphor and its variations on the eighteenth and nineteenth-century European consciousness.

In the rejection of this dream of uncramped creativity, Tennyson does two important things: he returns to the contrast between energetic flux and static timelessness, and he affirms, as his third agent for revitalization, his commitment to the superiority of Western European, Judeo-Christian culture. With a change of tone similar to but more intense than that signaled by the word "bluster" in line 63, Tennyson pronounces himself "fool" and condemns the moments spent in meditation on the "summer isles of Eden," this "Lotus land," as "the dream, the fancy," emphasizing that he "*know*[s] [his] words are wild . . . ," perhaps forgetting that he has also stated that "knowledge comes but wisdom lingers." Tennyson will have nothing to do with Zen, for indeed "wisdom" for the European must derive from a context in which the best in his culture has been accepted and absorbed. In this area, Tennyson anticipates Arnold, Eliot and all those who have stressed the essential role of "tradition" in the life of our culture and especially in the potential achievements of our poets. "Better fifty years of Europe than a cycle of Cathay" certainly represents, as does "I count the gray barbarian lower than the Christian child," European racism. The Victorians, however, would not have seen it this way or in these terms. Since there are few societies that have not created a philosophy and a rhetoric that champions both their best and worst, the historical context is important. In his belief in the superiority of Christian values and achievements, Tennyson was in familiar and articulate company.

But this need not be the emphasis at all. The importance of the European tradition is internalized in a way consistent with the poem as a whole and with its final, very personal, passage. This seeming emphasis on a contrast between the chosen Christian and the "squalid savage" appears less simplistic and more metaphorical when placed in the context of Tennyson's overwhelming concern with rejecting timelessness for time, so that he can connect himself to a tradition that will sustain him as poet. The Orient, Tennyson believes, rightly or not, has nothing to offer in the way of assistance for the European artist. A place without history cannot have a literary and cultural tradition that will provide inspiration and images. The "cycle of Cathay" represents an eternal circular movement. He cannot imagine incorporating this symbol into his art, though *Idylls of the King* has its own mythic circularity. Tennyson's use of myth in his own poetry is particularly both Victorian and personal in that often its original timelessness is put in the service of Victorian themes and modes emphasizing time, as in "Ulysses" or "Demeter and Persephone." Certainly in his usage the Oriental elements in Greek mythology are minimized. "The fifty years of Europe" are not years of material progress alone: they are the years of Blake, Wordsworth, Shelley, Keats, Byron, Browning, Tennyson, Arnold, and Dickens.

In the final section of the poem, Tennyson returns to the tradition of the Romantic meditative ode, pronouncing a prayerful invocation that connects the conclusion of "Locksley Hall" to the conclusion of "Frost at Midnight," "Tintern Abbey," and "To a Skylark." The invocation is to "Mother-Age," a previously undefined element, though a recent exegesis of the poem's imagery assumes that this refers to the contemporary ethos, "whose son he has pronounced himself to be." [10] The phrase "for mine I knew not" reinforces the orphan archetype introduced earlier, and the phrase "help me as when life began" suggests that her agency was of value in producing the energy and exhilaration of his youth that have been described earlier in the poem. "Mother-Age," however, is called on to "rift the hills, and roll the waters, flash the lightnings, weigh the sun," activities we could hardly expect from the materialistic contemporary ethos which Tennyson has so vigorously denounced earlier in the poem or even from "the ringing grooves of change." [11] Nor are these activities to be associated with the time when "the kindly earth shall slumber, lapt in universal law" or with the phrase "yet I doubt not thro' the ages one increasing purpose runs." Tennyson is appropriately ambiguous, but the clues do suggest that he is making an association between the inner "founts of inspiration" and an external agency whose actions will be both symbolic of the dynamism of his own creativity and representative of some principle of energy in the universe at large. The degradation of nature may have proceeded so far that this is mainly a Victorian analog of or even replacement for the more specific invocations of the guiding power and symbolic force of nature in earlier Romantic poetry. Perhaps Tennyson has purposefully sought an independent representation of the spiritual energy of the universe which the poet can call upon for inspiration and model. This agency is maternal, fruitful, ancient, and powerful. The immediate function of "Mother-Age" is to precipitate disturbances in the status quo of the external environment, invigorating the poet so that his energy from within will reawaken and join forces with the energy outside. Ultimately they will merge and the poet's creativity will be reborn. He has joined himself once again to the tradition—the "ancient founts of inspiration well thro' all my fancy yet"—and the need for rhetoric has disappeared.

The rediscovery of his creativity is followed immediately by a dismissal of concern with frustration and impotence: "Howsoever these things be, a long farewell to Locksley Hall." He tells us that no longer has he need for this landscape which has served its symbolic purpose in the poetic structure of his revitalization: "Now for me the woods may wither, now for me the roof-tree fall." Storm images climax the poem, variants of Wordsworth's "correspondent breeze," Shelley's "west wind," Coleridge's "Mad lutanist . . . that rav'st without, / Bare crag, or mountain-tairn, or blasted tree," perhaps ultimately of the whirlwind out of which speaks the awesome voice of cosmic mystery.

The problem of "Locksley Hall" still remains. Many readers have felt that Tennyson has had too facile a triumph over the despair which Wordsworth and Blake among the Romantics conquer, yet which Keats, Coleridge, and Byron, for different reasons of art and personality, cannot. Whereas Wordsworth's conquest comes from a convincing vision of nature, man, and the spiritual essence behind nature, Tennyson's victory comes, so critics have assumed, from action somehow polluted for the modern mind by the insensitivity and moral egoism of Victorian values and the racism and nationalism of the Crimean War. This weakness, however, is minimized if we see the poem at its most unconsciously prophetic, the record of the movement of a mind sincerely embracing values that have brought destruction in the belief that they would bring happiness. Yet it is not necessary, or even accurate, to see the poem in this way at all. As an alternative interpretation, "Locksley Hall" is a poem about "the act of the mind." For the blast, the thunderbolt, the "rain or hail, or fire or snow" are images of the poet's embracing the act of creation, his renewed commitment to a dynamic art. "Locksley Hall," then, is a fine but flawed poem in the Romantic tradition. In a sense, at this stage in his career, Tennyson knew less about poetry than the major Romantics, an inadequacy reflected in what he has to say about himself as poet and in the achievement of the poem.

All in all, the Romantic architecture or structure of "Locksley Hall" is more impressive than the seemingly Victorian interior ornamentation. Even the decoration reveals Tennyson's Romantic emphasis on his own sense of self and on the poem as a formal mode of the poet's self-exploration. "Locksley Hall" can be taken as emblematic of the development from Romantic to Victorian poetry, exemplifying the maxim that the more things change the more they remain the same. The pre-dominance of the lyric and direct utterance of Blake, Wordsworth, Coleridge, Keats, and Shelley falters as Tennyson, Browning, and Arnold gradually begin to wear the masks of dramatic narrative and monolog, as Tennyson has begun to do even in "Locksley Hall." But the major concern with self, though perhaps a weaker and less triumphant self, and the self as poetic process and poem, continues.

6

Woven Paces and Waving Hands

EXCEPT FOR "MORTE D'ARTHUR" (1842), which later became "The Passing of Arthur" (1869), "Merlin and Vivien" was the first composed of the twelve sections of *Idylls of the King*, and perhaps the best.[1] In theme and imagery it has more in common with "Locksley Hall" and "Merlin and the Gleam" than with the other *Idylls*. Standing almost midway in the span of Tennyson's long career, it suggests that throughout his poetry Tennyson is as concerned with himself as poet and with the creative process as with the war between sense and soul. It is representative of the best Victorian attempts to handle in narrative the themes the Romantics manifested in lyric structures.

The "Merlin and Vivien" episode has been misinterpreted by critics, though Tennyson himself, often quite misleading, has set the right direction in his remarks to his son that "in the story of 'Merlin and Nimue' I have read that Nimue means the Gleam,—which signifies in my poem the higher poetic imagination." [2] Of all the critics, only Gordon Haight has hinted at the relevance of this remark to "Merlin and Vivien," stressing the etymological-mythological origin of Nimue (Vivien) and explicating "Merlin and the Gleam." [3] However, "Merlin and Vivien" is also a poem about the artist and his creativity or imagination.[4] It is Tennyson's vision, in the context of a tradition which deals with the poet's frustration as poet that runs from Coleridge to Arnold, of the failure of the imagination to sustain creativity. Like the nightingale and what it represents, Vivien is a "deceiving elf."

Haight maintains that when Tennyson came to write "Merlin and the Gleam" there remained in his mind "simply the idea of the glimmering Welsh fairy,—now you see her, now you don't. It was obvious that he was not thinking at all of his evil and fleshly Vivien when he equated Nimue with 'the higher poetic imagination.' " [5] Nimue did not become "Vivien" until 1859. The final title, "Merlin and Vivien," was not applied until 1870. In 1856, the Idyll's title was "Merlin and Nimue," and in the trial edition of 1857 it was called "Nimue, or the True and the False." [6] Tennyson seems fully aware of the ambivalence of the name when writing "Nimue." For in this Idyll Merlin represents the poet, Tennyson himself, just as in "Merlin and the Gleam." [7] Vivien, however, represents the negative side of creativity or the imagination, the dark and destructive force in the poetic whirlwind. She is a projection of Merlin's melancholy, vanity, and frustration as artist. His defeat at her hands is a symbolic representation of the defeat of the imagination in the tradition of Romantic poetry. So "Merlin and Vivien" is not only about the war between sense and soul, between intellect and sloth, but about the failure of the poetic imagination. Merlin is the artist, not the intellect, and his defeat is an internal one.

Almost everything we know of Vivien, and most of what we know of Merlin, comes from the Idyll to which they give their names. Vivien appears briefly in "Guinevere" (ll. 25-29) and in

"Balin and Balan" (ll. 439-578), revealing herself, especially in the latter, to be an embodiment of cunning deceit and an advocate of the supremacy of physical reality. Unlike Merlin, few references are made to her by other characters in the poem. When she is there, she plays a role. Otherwise she fades into the unspecified background of general evil epitomized by the phrase "Mark's way." Merlin, however, plays a more pervasive role in the poem, as frequent reference is made to him in other *Idylls*, "The Coming of Arthur," "Gareth and Lynette," "The Holy Grail," "Pelleas and Ettare," "The Last Tournament," and "The Passing of Arthur." Indeed, despite his bewitched removal from Camelot early in the chronology of the *Idylls*, his former presence and achievements continue to influence heavily the atmosphere of Arthur's realm. His very absence is almost a presence, his disappearance a symbol of what has gone wrong.

In all references to Merlin, other than in "Merlin and Vivien," the great magician is the Kubla Khan of this Arthurian Xanadu. He has "decreed" Camelot into existence; he is the builder of this great city. Significantly, it has been built to music, associating the work and the work process with art and the creations of the imagination. Like Hephaestus or Vulcan or Mulciber, like the artist of Blake's poem who made both the tiger and the lamb, Merlin has fashioned the city and its interior, "our mighty hall, / Which Merlin built for Arthur long ago," described in "The Holy Grail," ll. 225-226. In "Gareth and Lynette" we are told that Merlin knows "all arts"; in the "Holy Grail" that he "moulded" a great statue. In "The Last Tournament" he is associated with "strange rhyme" and "mystic babble," the artist's traditional mastery of some secret language; in "The Passing of Arthur" with prophecy. Most revealingly, in "The Holy Grail" the artificer has made, we are told, a great chair:

> In our great hall there stood a vacant chair,
> Fashioned by Merlin ere he passed away . . .
>   "for there," he said,
> "No man could sit but should be lose himself."

> *And once by misadvertence Merlin sat*
> *In his own chair, and so was lost. . . .*
>
> (ll. 167-176)

So, indeed, in an episode other than "Merlin and Vivien," in a kind of analogical other version, Merlin's creation, his great chair, has been the instrument of his loss of himself and of his existence as artist. We are not given the circumstances of that strange "misadvertence." But the problem and the pattern are independent of Vivien the character. At any rate, it is evident that Tennyson's Merlin, both in mood and function, is similar to other Romantic and Victorian depictions of artists whose major battlegrounds are internal.

Like Coleridge's "Dejection: An Ode," with which it has much in common as a depiction of the positive and the negative powers of the imagination, "Merlin and Vivien" opens in the progressive form of the past tense with a storm threatening: "A storm was coming, but the winds were still." The scene, the "wild woods of Broceliande" in which "at Merlin's feet the wily Vivien lay," is dominated by "an oak, so hollow, huge, and old / It looked a tower of ivied masonwork. . . ." So the storm and the prison, two of the major symbols of the poem, are introduced in the opening short stanza, anticipating the amplification of both these elements into images of the creative spirit and its prison-house. The dialectic is a subtle one. At different stages in the poem Tennyson depicts the storm as both catalyst to Merlin's dormant and frustrated creative powers and as projection of those powers out of control; similarly, the prison-house is not Vivien's body but a special tensionless realm of complete flight from the storms of the imagination. Ironically, Vivien is to use the storm that breaks at the poem's conclusion as the instrument to persuade Merlin to "yield" her the charm (ll. 931-964). Unlike the storm of "Locksley Hall," the "act of the mind," this storm does not bring rebirth and revitalization but "peace; and what should not have been," and sleep. The overstrained and, for some readers, the unconvincing revitalization of the conclusion of "Locksley Hall," in "rain and hail, or fire or snow," has been followed roughly twenty years later by a false storm as well as a fallen artist. Though critics have commented on this process of disenchantment in Tennyson's career, of his gradual loss of faith in the beneficent mutuality of the poet and his time, and on his "tragic vision" in *Idylls of the King*,[8] "Merlin and Vivien" should be mentioned as a crucial text in this development.[9]

The storm and the prison, both existing *in potentia* at the opening of the poem, to be actualized in the final lines, are the background against which Tennyson explains the scene of the poem's beginning. The first five introductory lines are followed by 211 lines of flashback. We learn that Mark and Vivien, conspirators against Arthur's realm, have pledged themselves to translate their hate into action. Vivien has stolen into Camelot, ingratiated herself with Guinevere, attempted to make capital for dissension and psychological blackmail out of her knowledge of Guinevere's and Lancelot's love, and even attempted to seduce Arthur. Vivien's direct motivation for action is her hatred of the chaste and her desire for power. Her weapons are rumor, falsehood, slander, and blackmail, abetted by instinctive cunning; she can smell weakness no matter how distant. Like Merlin, she is an embodiment of the imagination, but of the perverse imagination, and a master of language, but of language that destroys rather than creates. Did Tennyson have Ulysses in mind when he referred to her as "the wily Vivien?" Regardless, Merlin seems the "other" Ulysses of Tennyson's poem, the hero who has indeed yielded.[10] Perhaps in "Merlin and Vivien" Tennyson was thinking of that traditional Ulysses, whom he had not emphasized earlier, the cunning, wily, treacherous, imaginative but anti-heroic manipulator of men. Just as there are two sides to the Greek hero, so there are two sides to Merlin, and one of them is Vivien.

Vivien seems to have almost no independent existence in the poem. She exists as a function of Merlin's melancholy. Though she acts and speaks in an independent way in the narrative, it is against a mythological background that de-emphasizes her substantiality as a character. In general, characters in *Idylls of the King* must fight the overpowering tide of allegory and personification if they are to have realistic credibility. However, Tennyson rarely wants them to.

Some put up a battle, but Vivien hardly at all. Consequently, critics have complained that she is too blatantly and unrelievedly an embodiment of evil. Yet the kind of evil she embodies is extremely important for an understanding of the poem. That she is an allegorical personification is completely consistent with and necessary to the poetic vision of the poem as a whole. She is a personification of the negative side of Merlin the poet and of the creative imagination. Thus, "Merlin and Vivien" is an allegory about the struggle between two aspects of the artist.[11] Despite Vivien's subversive role in Camelot, "sowing one ill hint from ear to ear . . . they heard and let her be" (l. 144). Soon after, "the wily Vivien stole from Arthur's court." Rather than continuing to bring us to the present, the narrative returns to the past again, describing Vivien's attempt, before she had left the court, to seduce Arthur and "to gain" the love of Merlin. In a sense, the narrative makes use of the past, of an analog of memory, in a way similar to the use of memory in the Romantic meditative ode; there is the same constant movement back and forth, emphasizing different degrees of pastness, and underlining both the failure of the past to vitalize the present and the importance of using the past to understand the present. Lines 1-5 are in the present; lines 6-144 describe the past activities of Vivien from her pledge to Mark to destroy Camelot to her departure from Arthur's court, omitting, however, the description of her attempt to seduce Arthur and "to gain" Merlin; lines 187-194 describe Merlin's mood following his growing tolerance of Vivien; and line 195 resumes the movement towards the present begun in the earlier description of Vivien's departure from the court (ll. 144-147), for lines 195-216 describe the journey of Merlin and Vivien to Broceliande. Circuitously, we have reached the present of the opening lines of the poem. There are to be other returns to the past or flashbacks in the remainder of the Idyll, but they are relatively minor and predominately illustrative, not explanatory. As in the Romantic meditative ode, so too in "Merlin and Vivien," despite its narrative form, the mood of the present can mainly be explained, and perhaps even changed, by an exploration of the past. While the narrative pattern demands that a good deal of the action be externalized, the emphasis on the relationship between past and present is built into a structural pattern that in its flexible handling of time has much in common with a traditional Romantic form whose major theme is the artist's concern with his own creativity.

Vivien, having failed in her attempt to seduce Arthur, turns to Merlin, who is neither an embodiment of chastity nor of goodness, but who is described as the man of experience, the Prospero of Camelot, and even the Shakespeare who lies behind Prospero, the creator of the entire aery kingdom and the tempest itself. While Arthur has immortality in a mythic pattern, Merlin, the Idyll emphasizes, has "fame." He is "the most famous man of all those times." It is mainly this fame that his self-betrayal is to deprive him of at the poem's conclusion. He is to be "lost to life and use and name and fame" (l. 967), attributes of the artist rather than the king—existence in mortal form, productivity or creativity, individuality, and recognition. The description of Vivien's initial attempt to ingratiate herself with Merlin is prefaced by the longest description in the *Idylls* of Merlin's powers, emphasizing his knowledge of all the arts, his constructive capacity as artisan, his prophetic powers, and his magical ability, artist, artisan, seer, and verbal prestidigitator. Is it too much to see a partial Tennyson self-portrait in these lines? [12]

Vivien's plan of seduction has scant success. Her charms succeed only in producing Merlin's amused tolerance of her presence. She is only "half-disdained." Her flattery of "the old man" is "felt" and at times he "would half believe her true . . . and so the seasons went." Whatever attractions Vivien has for the magician come from his inner needs. Yet, her attractions seem minor up to this point. The serious threat that Vivien is to offer to Merlin's existence as artist comes suddenly as a result of changed conditions within Merlin. Vivien's destructive potential becomes actualized only after and as a result of Merlin's loss of faith in himself and what he has built, his previous positive and healthy imaginative faculties polluted with "a great melancholy . . . with dreams and darkness" (ll. 187-188). In this sense, Vivien as "the gray marauder," associated with "doom," "ever-moaning battle in the mist,/ World-war of dying flesh . . . / Death in all life" (ll. 189-192), has no existence independent of Merlin's divided imagination. The Merlin

who made this city "built to music" should be able to offer major
resistance to "Mark's way," which Vivien seems to represent in the
poem. But "leaving Arthur's court," Merlin goes to the beach, em-
barks, "and Vivien follow[s] but he mark[s] her not" (l. 197). She
inevitably and irrepressibly goes with him, a condition of his melancholy, not the cause of it, and a projection of his imagination. The
shock for the reader is in how little real resistance he offers to her in
the rest of the poem.

Merlin's abdication of initiative to Vivien, whatever she represents, is clear as soon as they enter the boat, for "she took the helm
and he the sail" (l. 198). The threatening storm has not descended
yet, but the still wind of the opening line of the poem, postdating
the moment of the embarkation, for we are still in flashback, has
been preceded by a "sudden wind" which drove the boat "across
the deeps." We have been given no explanation for Merlin's capitulation, and the connivance of the "sudden wind" suggests a
magical manipulation within an internal drama. Significantly, for
the first time in the Idyll, the charm is introduced, and the minor
reference to the image of the prison in lines 3-4 is amplified in some
detail. Merlin and Merlin's Vivien, copilots, one at the helm, the
other at the sail, in flight from melancholy and impotence, have directed themselves to the place where the prison image will become
dominant and real. That Merlin once had told her of the charm (l.
203) in some less vulnerable past emphasizes the difference between the Merlin before and after "the great melancholy" which
preceded the images of death and faithlessness. It is important to
remember that to Merlin the melancholy is a condition prior to his
vision of the destruction of Camelot. This seems a genuine puzzle,
as "Merlin and Vivien" certainly is also about the defeat of Arthurian Christian values by inner corruption of the senses and by internal evil. Yet this early Idyll, despite its later extensive revisions and
lengthening, seems at critical points to direct our attention to Merlin as artist and to Merlin's struggle as an interior one between two
aspects of his own imagination and creative powers. Merlin is an
artist in search of his own prison, a variant of "the palace of art"
and Locksley Hall, combined with the psychological ambiance of
the death wish that permeates "Tithonus" and appears, for exam-

ple, in "In Memoriam," "Ulysses," and "Maud." Tennyson vividly depicts the kind of living-death that the perverse imagination ever seeks to impose upon the creative imagination:

> The man so wrought on ever seem'd to lie
> Closed in the four walls of a hollow tower,
> From which there was no escape for evermore;
> And none could find that man for evermore,
> Nor could he see but him who wrought the charm
> Coming and going, and he lay as dead
> And lost to life and use and name and fame.
> (ll. 206-212)

Wordsworth's "prison-house," Coleridge's playful "Lime-tree Bower my Prison," Blake's "cage," Browning's "dark tower," Dickens's "bleak house," Shaw's "heartbreak-house," and Kafka's "castle," to name but a few, are images in the same tradition.

The exploration of the narrative past of the poem suddenly ends on line 216, and we are returned to its first lines, the scene in the dark forest before the huge oak where Vivien "lay . . . all her length and kiss'd his feet, / As if in deepest reverence and in love" (ll. 217-218). However, Baum unquestionably is correct when he states that Merlin does not "fall victim . . . to the snares of the flesh," [13] though the capitulation is usually interpreted this way.[14] Baum offers flattery as the efficacious snare, but claims that this "is not what the allegory demands." [15] However, neither sex nor flattery finally destroy Merlin. It is Vivien herself, in the "tender rhyme of 'trust me not at all or all in all' " which she once "heard the great Lancelot sing," who makes clear the nature of the conflict between these two adversaries and who points to the source of her power over Merlin:

> " 'It is the little rift within the lute,
> That by and by will make the music mute,
> And ever widening slowly silence all.' "
> (ll. 388-390)

Like Coleridge in "Dejection: An Ode," so too Tennyson through
the words of Vivien's song, originally Lancelot's, uses the lute to
represent the creative powers or the imagination. But there is a "little rift within the lute." In this case, certainly, the lute is Merlin,
who built an entire city to music. The "rift" refers to Merlin's
weakness, to his vulnerability, to the "great melancholy" which represents the negative potential of his creativity, the wind that can
roar out of control and destroy the creation and the creator, of
which Vivien is the prophet if not the embodiment. The rift within
Merlin exists prior to Vivien's attempt to widen it through sensuality. Merlin's complete destruction can come only when he commits
himself fully to that aspect of himself that Vivien represents.

The long central section of the Idyll contains the modifications of this on-going dialectic as Vivien searches for the method
and the words that will accomplish Merlin's complete self-capitula-
tion. At first, the playful Vivien is unable to allay Merlin's suspi-
cions, but gains his thanks for breaking up his melancholy, suggesting that the illness of spirit from which he suffers is not so
permanently intense that he cannot continue through a series of
ups and downs, of movement from relative depression to normalcy
and back to depression again. Vivien makes much of her efforts to
assist him, and Merlin explains his unapproachability by comparing
his feelings of the previous days to lying "upon the shore" as a wave
is about to break. The image suggests madness and suicide, echoing
"through a glass darkly":

> Even such a wave, but not so pleasurable,
> Dark in the glass of some presageful mood,
> Had I for three days seen, ready to fall.
> (ll. 292-294)

Vivien chooses to interpret this mood as "mistrustful," sign of his
continued and renewed unwillingness to give her the keys to the
prison, the secret of the charm: "O Merlin, teach it me. / The
charm so taught will charm us both to rest." The Ulysses figure
who "cannot rest from travel" is being serenaded by an inner voice
and need that glorifies the pleasures of "to pause, to make an end,

/ To rust unburnished, not to shine in use!" ("Ulysses," ll. 22-23). Later in the poem Merlin is to emphasize that "I rather dread the loss of use than fame" (l. 517). Merlin's "use," of course, is as the maker of things, the artist and the artificer, who previously has been commited to "the act of the mind." On Merlin's maintaining that he has trusted Vivien "too much," she sings the foreboding song of Lancelot, to which Merlin replies with the story of "the song that once I heard / By this huge oak" (ll. 403-404) and the chase of the hart with golden horns. Obviously, the oak did not threaten to be a prison then, the singers were powerful and ener- getic, the song was "noble," and the chase after the hart with golden horns is a fable about the joys of energetically pursuing the unattainable, the artist in search of his greatness. As in "Merlin and the Gleam," here too they "chased the *flashes* of his golden horns / Until they vanished by the fairy well" (ll. 225-226). Merlin com- pares that "noble," life-expanding song to Vivien's which suggests to him that she knows already "this cursed charm, / . . . and that I lay / And felt them slowly ebbing, name and fame" (ll. 433-435).

Vivien then argues that fame should be subordinate to love. Ironically, though she is the embodiment of falsehood and rumor, she states that since Merlin is assumed to be "the master of all art" he is also rumored to be "master of all vice" (ll. 465-467). Conse- quently, he should renounce fame for love. Merlin revises the text to read "rather use than fame," and, in a long passage with autobio- graphical echoes, presents the Tennysonian and nineteenth-century emphasis upon the process rather than the product, saying "fame with men" is "but ampler means to serve mankind." Echoing "Ulysses," line 43, "He works his work, I mine," Merlin says that he "needs must work my work," again suggesting that Tennyson means us to see the failure of Merlin partially as an antinomy to the success of the hero of the earlier poem. The "fame" that Tennyson earlier in his career had found so double-edged, and to which he was so sensitive, must be accepted only for the opportuni- ties it brings to increase "use." The irony of the poem is, of course, that the assault from within renders Merlin useless in the end. To give Vivien power through the charm, in this curious allegory, will deprive Merlin of all power and end his creativity.

Vivien jokingly retorts that he clings to the charm to protect his harem of "buxom captives" in a series of towers with four walls "all about this world." Merlin, amused but unshaken, tells the story of the origin of the charm in which a reluctant magician provides his king perforce with the charm "which, being wrought upon the queen / Might keep her all his own." This magician seems an analog to the Romantic hermit

> *Who lived alone in a great wild on grass,*
> *Read but one book, and ever reading grew*
> *So grated down and filed away with thought,*
> *So lean his eyes were monstrous . . .*
> *And since he kept his mind on one sole aim,*
> *Nor ever touch'd fierce wine, nor tasted flesh,*
> *Nor own'd a sensual wish, to him the wall*
> *That sunders ghosts and shadow-casting men*
> *Became a crystal, and he saw them thro' it,*
> *And heard their voices talk behind the wall,*
> *And learnt their elemental secrets, powers*
> *And forces. . . .*
>
>   (ll. 619-630)

After satisfying the king's demand, the hermit

> *Went back to his old wild, and lived on grass,*
> *And vanish'd, and his book came down to me.*
>   (ll. 647-648)

In reply to Vivien's remark on the similarity between the magician of the fable and Merlin, the latter emphasizes, "Nay, not like to me," insisting that physically they are quite different. But the major difference is in their powers. Whereas the magician of the fable could read the book containing the charm, Merlin says that

> *none can read the text, not even I;*
> *And none can read the comment but myself;*
> *And in the comment did I find the charm.*
>   (ll. 679-681)

The essential comparison is between the uncorrupted imaginative power of the magician of the fable and the comparatively lesser powers of Merlin. The fable basically is presented as Merlin's own creation, and seems a quasi-mythological-etiological projection of his awareness of the difference between his former and his present powers or, at least, in the tradition of the Romantic meditative ode, of the idea or feeling that he has of this difference. Significantly, in the fable, the king uses the charm upon the queen, just as Merlin is to use it through Vivien upon himself, "and he lay as dead, / And lost all use of life." It is not necessary to push the psychological concept of the divided but once united self into every aspect of the poem, but certainly the use of the image of royal unity divided into conflict between its constituent parts reinforces the motif of Merlin's divided imagination. The book that contains the charm in its commentary is like some ancient Talmudic scroll, a primitive calligraphy condensed in the margins in "a language that has long gone by," not to speak of the awesome inscrutability of the text. Even the mysterious book is divided into two parts. The association of Merlin with this great work reinforces the reader's association of Merlin with some master artist, some Prospero-Shakespeare, as close to the deepest mysteries as man will ever come.

Merlin still will not trust in Vivien, suggesting that she might "assay it on some one of the Table-Round, / And all because ye dream they babble of you." Consequently, in lines 689-803, Vivien unleashes an embittered hysterical "defaming and defacing" attack on Sir Valence, Sir Sagramore, Sir Percivale, Sir Lancelot, and Arthur. Though her tirade is catalyzed by Merlin's fear of her hostility to the Round Table, and there is some appropriateness in her passionate demonstration of that hostility, the response seems overlong and, at best, a dramatic representation of the notion that Vivien embodies false language and the perverse imagination; at worst, an inappropriate tactic that Vivien has already been made to seem clever enough to avoid. Yet perhaps this is part of the genius of the dialectic between these two magicians: Vivien has not had and will not have any argumentative success on the level of logic, or ethics, or rhetorical persuasion. This letting loose of her passion in a way that normally would completely confound an argument based on persuasive factors in the long run proves the most successful tactic she could have devised. For Merlin is never persuaded to give her the charm. He is simply outlasted and "overworn." Vivien's attacks upon the "Table-Round" and Camelot, despite Merlin's knowledge of the beginning of corruption and the ruin that is to come, do not undermine his confidence in the essential goodness and nobility of his and Arthur's creations, though indeed his rebuttal on their behalf places more emphasis on the excuse than on the fact. Vivien's attack on Arthur produces "loathing" in Merlin to the extent that Vivien, believing "Merlin overborne,"

> *By instance, recommenced, and let her tongue*
> *Rage like a fire among the noblest names. . . .*
> (ll. 799-800)

But she seriously miscalculates. Merlin still has the strength and the will to condemn her vilification and reaffirm the danger of telling her the charm. Clearly, Vivien's miscalculation has not been one of persuasive argument but of relative will power. "Deeming Merlin overborne," she has anticipated a victory still some moments away.

To make the irony of his final capitulation most effective, Tennyson has Merlin himself make absolutely clear that he has not been deceived or persuaded by Vivien's vilification. In lines 807-836, Merlin condemns Vivien as "plotter," "harlot," "flatterer," and concludes, "I am weary of her," though, significantly, as if he cannot muster the voice and the will to make his private imaginative pronouncements public and effective, "he spoke in words part heard, in whispers part. . . ." On hearing the word "harlot," Vivien rises as if to kill him, then falsely "[takes] / To bitter weeping like a beaten child," and claims again that she has sacrificed her reputation to her love for him. All her darkening of others, she claims, has been to make him seem brighter. The dialectic comes to an end as Vivien, compared to a snake, turns away. Suddenly that quiescent storm, so long in coming, promises finally to break. The image that Tennyson uses is one of reconciliation—"And the dark wood grew darker toward the storm / In silence . . ."—to prepare the way for Merlin's attempt at reconciliation with Vivien and to contrast with the separation that is to come. Merlin's "anger slowly died / Within him, till he let his wisdom go / For ease of heart, and *half* believed her true. . . ." Ironically, he calls "her to shelter in the hollow oak" that is to become his permanent prison; she rejects his advances, and proclaims that

> *what was once to me*
> *Mere matter of the fancy, now hath grown*
> *The vast necessity of heart and life,*
> (ll. 921-923)

and calls upon heaven to bring down justice on her if she has ever schemed against his peace. The storm explodes.

What to the modern reader might be an untenable imposition of the divine is made quite acceptable and effective by associating the storm not with the divine but with the natural and the malevolent. It is not an instrument of divinity in some ordered and just universe, though Vivien for a moment fears that "heaven had heard her oath." The Judeo-Christian tradition of the "divine," of the voice of god or justice speaking from the midst of the storm or the whirlwind, is absent completely. The storm is a negative image of chaos and of imagination out of control. Whereas the storms in "Locksley Hall" and "Maud" are symbols of imaginative commitment, this storm is neither a reaction of a just heaven, destroying the evil Vivien, nor a symbol of the reawakening of Merlin's creative powers. Ironically, it truly frightens Vivien into Merlin's arms; she calls for his protection, remembers her purpose, and uses the storm to defeat Merlin completely. For Merlin "raised his eyes and saw / The tree that shone white-listed thro' the gloom" (ll. 936-937), suggesting some special relationship, which has been anticipated in the first lines of the poem, between the storm and the tree, potential imaginative revitalization and the potential prison-house of the imagination. The vivid flash highlights the choice.

But Merlin seems hardly to have a choice at all. For him, the storm is ambivalent. The great Romantic image of rebirth of the creative imagination, the correspondent breeze, has its destructive side. Vivian and the storm are one. The imagination has its perverseness, its desire to embrace death, timelessness, and peace. Its potential for evil and destructiveness, its delight in peculiar perversities, can overcome its positive strengths. Out of hand, the imagination can be a breeding ground of morbid fancies, of sexual phantasm, of deep and self-destructive melancholy, of psychological nightmares. While "overhead / Bellow'd the tempest; and the rotten branch snapt," Merlin and Vivien grasp one another,

> *Till now the storm, its burst of passion spent,*
> *Moaning and calling out of other lands,*
> *Had left the ravaged woodland yet once more*
> *To peace. . . .*
>
> (ll. 954-962)

In a manner consistent with many of his other poems, Tennyson combines illicit sexual fulfillment and the death wish against a turbulent landscape or physical background to represent his ultimate vision of hell, the end of energy, the end of "use." Merlin, aware of his inner self-defeat, "overtalk'd and overworn, / Had yielded. . . ." The great artificer is simply tired and cannot endure; his mind is unpersuaded, but his will is broken. Immediately Vivien

> *put forth the charm*
> *Of woven paces and of waving hands,*
> *And in the hollow oak he lay as dead,*
> *And lost to life and use and name and fame.*
>
> (ll. 965-968)

7

Browning's Painter in Wasteland

THE MOST TERRIFYING depiction in nineteenth-century poetry of the Romantic theme of the failure of the imagination and the impotence of the artist is in Browning's "Andrea del Sarto." Whether or not this great poem contains significant biographical elements cannot be resolved adequately.[1] Yet, Browning early in his career glorified Shelley into an archetype of the kind of intuitive and subjective poet he himself was not and he believed his wife was; and throughout his career regret arose about the role he had chosen for himself.[2] There is no evidence to support the assumption that Browning identified his wife with Lucrezia, but there is some minor evidence to suggest that he identified some part of himself with Andrea. Regardless of the elusive psychological component, Andrea

94

del Sarto is Browning's most vivid depiction of the failed artist in the Romantic tradition, despite the obvious victory of Browning's characteristically Victorian desire to objectify, represented by the dramatic monolog form. The poem's imagery and structure connect it, on the one hand, to Romantic poems concerning the failure of the poet's confidence in his powers and his mission, and, on the other, to wasteland poems of the nineteenth and twentieth centuries.[3]

Browning apostrophized Shelley in the frequently quoted phrase from *Pauline*: "Sun-treader, life and light be thine forever!"[4] Everywhere in Browning's poetry sunlight and daytime are associated with imagination and life; and, in a curious reversal of the typical pattern of Romantic imagery, the paraphernalia of the night, the moon, twilight, shadows, the color silver, dark gardens, yet not stars, are associated with the death of creativity and the failure of imagination. In *Paracelsus*, Browning presents the traditional Romantic comparison of youth to a strong fountain or river which, as time passes, ebbs into comparative impotence. He makes explicit a typical nineteenth-century extension of the metaphor by further modifying the river and fountain image with an explicit simile. This vehicle highlights Browning's concern with failed creativity:

> *I heard it in my youth when first*
> *The waters of my life outburst:*
> *But, now their stream ebbs faint, I hear*
> *That voice, still low, but fatal-clear—*
> *As if all poets, God ever meant*
> *Should save the world, and therefore lent*
> *Great gifts to, but who, proud, refused*
> *To do his work, or lightly used*
> *Those gifts, or failed through weak endeavor. . . .*
> (Pt. 2, ll. 235-243)

Robert Preyer makes much of this general point: "Browning . . . suffered intermittently all his life from the conviction that he had somehow sold his poetic birthright."[5] If he was not to be a Shelley, he was also not to be an Andrea, though it is not completely unreasonable to suggest that some of the success of "Andrea del Sarto" derives from the ability of Browning to empathize with the failed artist in a way that had been conditioned by his life and art between 1833 and 1855.

Browning's debt to Vasari, while great, has proved misleading more often than not. The poet's habitual work patterns and exploitations of source material have inspired scholars and critics not only to search for the original of a character or a story, but have suggested that only realistic interpretations of "Andrea del Sarto" and similar poems are feasible.[6] For obvious reasons, explicitly symbolic, if not allegorical, poems like "Childe Roland" escape this straitjacket. "Andrea" should be given such liberty as well, or at least the liberating attempt should be made, for despite the realistic assumptions of the dramatic monolog form and in the light of recent emphasis on the importance of the lyrical element in dramatic monologs,[7] it should be seen in the nineteenth-century tradition of poems that against a symbolic landscape dramatize the internal conflict of the poet's concern with his own creativity. This aspect of the poem has been so neglected that only one critic has stressed that Lucrezia is mainly a creation of Andrea's needs.[8]

The structure of failed self-justification gives the poem its psychological impressiveness, paralleling the attempt by Keats and Coleridge to capture in the structure of their odes the movement of their imaginations towards affirmation and rebirth. Andrea's mind spars with the reality of failure in an attempt to make it appear success. Like a fighter who has already intimated defeat in his defensive posture, it is quite evident that his movements forward and backwards, from hope of triumph to acknowledgment of failure, from present to future and from present to past, carry, in combination with the poem's wasteland imagery, the major experience Browning desires to depict. Even more than most dramatic monologs, the structure of "Andrea del Sarto" reflects the mind of its main character because the poem takes the pattern of its structure from the movement of his mind. On the deepest level, his mind is absolutely static. He knows very well that things will be as they are, as he had made them. On another level, his mind is in the process of exploring the possibilities of adjusting to its staticism. Browning's model for this more likely is in Keats, Coleridge, and Shelley than in Vasari.

There are, of course, certain correspondences between the movement of Andrea's self-justifying thoughts and his rhetoric. His 266-line monolog divides rather naturally into a number of parts. Precisely how many is a matter of interpretation, since a great deal of the success of the poem results from Browning's ability to create a sense of continuous mental flow, while at the same time distinguishing within the flow separate movements, all of which relate to the main pattern.[9]

Certainly the poem, like most dramatic monologs, attempts to persuade, though in the case of "Andrea del Sarto" there are three parties to be convinced. On the literal level, Andrea desires to persuade Lucrezia to remain with him, though he mostly recognizes the impossibility of the task. His argument also is directed outward towards the unacknowledged audience, the readers of the poem, though indeed the persuasion is of a most delicate kind; it is Browning's attempt to make us feel his poem's strength. Most important for the poem's inner tension, Andrea attempts to convince himself that responsibility for his failure as artist is not his own and, failing that, he must adjust to the situation that his character has created. While conscious rhetoric does not play the dominant role that it does, for example, in "The Bishop Orders His Tomb," the dramatic monolog form in general, unlike the lyric, is an attempt by author through character to persuade the audience of the credibility and meaningfulness of the speaker. As a negative example, the other side of the coin of Childe Roland, Andrea is entombed permanently in a wasteland of rhetoric and imagery through which he can only occasionally see and which is the most distinctive characterizing element in the poem. Roma King has commented that "The complex sentences, the numerous subordinations, the interpolations, the exclamations, the lack of syntactical connections give the effect of thought in conflict, of intellectual uncertainty and emotional instability. Andrea's aim is self-justification, but since he has not ordered his thinking, he cannot proceed straightforwardly. . . ."[10] But there is more to the structural problem of the poem than this. Andrea is primarily a man of blunted if not dead feelings who has substituted rhetoric and intellectual deviation for emotion. Andrea sees but does "not feel, how beautiful they are." [11]

The emotional twists of the poem are a graph of its basic structure. The frequent references to passivity, willessness, and calm of the opening of the poem continue for fifty lines, as if Browning had expanded the mood that Arnold was to encapsule in the first five lines of "Dover Beach," which has other parallels with "Andrea," especially the echos of "come from the window, love" ("Andrea," l. 210 and "let us but love each other: ("Andrea," l. 219) in "come to the window, sweet is the night-air" and "Ah, love, let us be true / To one another!" Certainly both poems are about the loss of emotional and artistic enthusiasm in a world of external and internal betrayal.[12] The first moment of emphasized emotion in "Andrea" breaks the mood of descriptive emptiness, the evening, autumn scene of the poem's opening. Andrea actually feels strongly. Of course, what he feels, what he wants to emphasize, is the responsibility of some external agent for his present situation. Andrea makes a pronouncement of self-justifying determinism. Unlike the Arnold of "To Marguerite—Continued," who expresses his sense of non-specificity of responsibility when he offhandedly comments that "a god, a god their severance ruled," Andrea quite positively at this point says: "So free we seem, so fettered fast we are! / I feel he [God] laid the fetter: let it lie!" (ll. 51-52). The description of the "common grayness" has been followed by an ascription of responsibility for this death in life, this earthly purgatory. Andrea has emotion for self-justification but for nothing else.

In the next section, Andrea turns directly to Lucrezia to defend the situation for which God is responsible, and, as a logical-rhetorical strategy, this abdication is quite consistent with the ambivalence of Andrea's position. He will strike out in as many different directions as promise some possibility of successful self-justification and shifting of blame, while, at the same time, impressing the reader that these are partially conscious, partially unconscious strategies which cannot even persuade the speaker. Andrea's general lack of emotion in this section reinforces the fact, ostensible in the poem's first words, of his capitulation of that aspect of himself that Lucrezia represents. At the same time, he reserves a degree of emotion for combative defense of an aspect of his art that he clearly admits to be inferior in its superiority. Andrea himself is never deceived by the "faultless[ness]," the perfectionism of his art. In defending himself, he is both consciously sophistical and honestly aware of his limitations. The two points of emotion between lines 53 and 77 are defenses of his craftsmanship. When he says "Behold Madonna!—I am bold to say I can do with my pencil" and comments that he can do what others "strive to do, and agonize to do, / And fail in doing," he is simply distinguishing himself from the multitude of the untalented without ever claiming that he is equal to the great. Indeed, the next section explicitly proclaims the gap between craftsmanship and genius. Certainly the level of his emotion is kept damped by his awareness of the failure of his creativity and imagination.

The poem has moved from description of the emotionless landscape of despair to a small peak of defensive emotion that introduces the long central section of the poem (ll. 77-144). Andrea's pronouncement of God's responsibility for his failure is followed by a brief shift of blame to Lucrezia, hardly a feasible strategy within the argumentative-persuasive context of Andrea's most obvious purpose: to persuade Lucrezia to remain at home that evening. Her carelessness in regard to his paintings is quickly subordinated to his recognition that his technical superiority hardly compensates for the lack of spiritual and aesthetic tension. In the language of deprivation, he remarks that those who strive "do much less, so much less, Someone says, / . . . Well, less is more, Lucrezia: I am judged" (ll. 76-78). Andrea's instincts are sound, as Browning will have them, for neither he nor his readers are to be permitted to escape the conclusion that external failure, when adequately defined, is the result of an internal condition. It seems impossible to imagine that Browning could have worked mainly in any form other than the dramatic monolog. What better way to manifest the relationship between condition and cause than through a form which depends upon depicting present psychological condition in terms of character as revealed in an expression that connects the present with the past?

That "there burns a truer light of God in them," Andrea clearly recognizes in a lengthy statement in which, as he strains to pull his failure out of the fire, there is a revealing disparity between his rhetorical assertions and the emotionlessness of his words and voice. In a tone of neutrality Andrea proclaims that, in essence, his works ascend to heaven and he remains earthbound, while the works of others remain earthbound while they ascend. The ascension of the artist seems to refer to an intensification of emotion and feeling, an exhilaration connected with the process of creativity rather than with the product, though indeed Andrea remarks that other artists have "sudden blood," are sensitive to criticism, while he is "unmoved by men's blame / Or their praise either." In presenting a true distinction, Andrea has convinced himself of the validity of a false distinction through a play on words, common in Browning's poetry, in which "earth" stands for "heaven" and the reverse. Yet, neither Andrea nor his works ascend and the play on words, used so successfully by Browning in the "success-failure-heaven-earth" vocabulary of "The Last Ride Together," falters and loses effectiveness in the face of Andrea's double failure. The distinction made by Browning's normal reversal of the terms is inapplicable to a failure so complete and so final that alternatives, even metaphoric ones, are irrelevant. All Andrea can do is to stress his craftsmanship and take his stand on the grounds of this minor achievement, as well as muster whatever little emotion is available to him. He is aware, however, of how minor and noncompensatory it is, just as he is aware, as he turns to his other catalyst of emotion in this central section of the poem, that, ultimately, even Lucrezia is not to blame in any personal sense for his failure.

To attack Lucrezia is to attack himself. If he must attack himself, he prefers to do so on other grounds. Had she given him "soul, / We might have risen to Rafael," he admits to be a senseless statement in which he is mainly personifying in Lucrezia an aspect of his own imagination with which he has failed to deal satisfactorily. If indeed Lucrezia had brought more "perfection," even a perfect "mind," the poem implies that Andrea's failure would not be less, but even more. His notion, "I might have done it for you," he quickly dismisses. All that he can imagine is that Lucrezia could have been more and better than she is already, again suggesting that Andrea's artistic sterility has found its perfect exterior symbol in Lucrezia's perfection. The only improvement he can imagine in his vision of Lucrezia is an increase in her perfection and its extension to other areas of personality. Would this have improved Andrea's art or his craftsmanship? Andrea's retreat is immediate. Paradoxically, the false and self-justifying argument that assuages moves through a syllogism that most readers feel represents Browning's voice speaking through Andrea's. "Incentives come from the soul's self," Andrea admits, suggesting that he recognizes that the ascension of the artist is always single, that the artistic venture is a personal one; its loneliness compensated only by the exhilaration of the process and the sublimity of the result. Like all "trips," the experience is noncommunal. Andrea, however, can accept this responsibility only against the background of a higher scapegoat. Returning to the self-justifying determinism of the poem's second section he concludes that "all is as God over-rules" and, at the end, "God compensates . . . punishes." The emotional graph as structure has charted Andrea's movement from emotionless retreat to painful confrontation. On the one hand, emotion and feeling have increased comparatively to the point where Andrea now must retreat again; on the other, the emotional level is much lower than what we would expect it to be, given these causes. Browning is able to make subtle variations on the Romantic hell and the Victorian purgatory—the heart that does not feel. Andrea finds relief in hard work and in the golden past, the former a Victorian existential commitment, the latter both a Romantic and Victorian myth that the Victorians had much the greater difficulty in sustaining.

The fourth section of the poem (ll. 145-172) details Andrea's happier days, "that long festal year at Fountain-bleau," patronized and appreciated by Francis I. The return to the golden past, and its comparison to the silver-gray present, so predominant a structural and imagistic technique in the tradition of the Romantic ode, plays an important role in highlighting the always existent gap between

Andrea's vision of success and his failure. Whereas Wordsworth uses the dip into the past to make meaningful and to renew the present and, consequently, creates an ideal past which can inspire the present, Browning creates a past in which Andrea reveals that the limits of his vision even then are connected directly to the failure that amounts to his life. For Wordsworth in "Tintern Abbey" and for Tennyson in "Locksley Hall," the distinguishing characteristic of the past is its fullness of feeling, its emotional content and the truths of the heart. In actuality, Andrea's "golden" days, anticipating, as Roma King suggests, the commercial images Andrea uses in the final section to depict his relationship with Lucrezia, are distinguished by his delusion that patronage, financial and social success, are related to artistic success.[13] Andrea, however, admits that even then he could only "*sometimes* leave the ground, / Put on the glory, Rafael's daily wear" (my italics). Though this is the one incident in the poem in which Andrea's tone suggests genuine happiness in the past and partial gladness in recollecting that time, Browning's readers are certainly given reason to feel that the grounds of this happiness and emotion are radically tainted. That the infection is within Andrea, and was within him then, is made clear when Andrea again explains his apostasy by referring to Lucrezia. Never is an outside agent other than Lucrezia or God, who play similar projective roles in the poem, responsible for Andrea's actions. "And had you not grown restless?" Andrea asks, and he concludes, "How could it end in any other way? / You called me, and I came home to your heart" (ll. 170-171). That he did not stay is compensated by Andrea's purgatorial delimiting of his personality and shrinking of his needs. By assuming that since he "reached it ere the triumph, what is lost," he is the ultimate stoic who accepts complete negation as a triumph. Certainly Browning has reversed the Romantic use of the return to the past in a significant way: lyric possibilities have become dramatic actualities, and the past is a road back to the condition of the present. The journey reveals that character remains essentially the same.

As if to emphasize this point, Browning has Andrea return to the past in a reprise of the same comparisons between himself and other artists that he had made in the poem's third section. In the

fifth section, to make the structural parallel obvious, Andrea moves
from consideration of his relative merits as painter to a high point
of emotion and aspiration almost identical with that in the third
section (ll. 111-115) in which what he almost dared to do earlier he
now actually does:

> *I hardly dare . . . yet, only you to see,*
> *Give the chalk here—quick, thus the line*
>   *should go!*
>   (ll. 195-196)

The quality of this daring, so unlike the "dare frame thy fearful
symmetry" of "The Tyger," has been conditioned and anticipated
by the failure to act earlier and the admission of the clear failure of
the action attempted now. Blake's artist-creator unhesitatingly
dares to frame or create the full and complete work of art, the
"fearful symmetry" which is itself a metaphor for all creation. He is
characterized as "immortal." Browning's artist, however, with quivering trepidation, hesitatingly, "hardly" dares to modify one line of
the full canvas created by someone else. The decisive, steady, and
continuous "immortal hand or eye" has become the indecisive,
quick, and sporadic hand of the artist so fallible in his perfectionism that he pathetically must call upon God and necessity to justify
his failures rather than create God as a projection of his own confidence and success. "Ay, but the soul! he's Rafael! rub it out," Andrea proclaims.

Certainly the movement of Andrea's mind from section three
to section five has revealed no alteration in his character. The structural parallelism simply emphasizes the staticism of his character
and art. The pride he takes in the compliments that have been paid
his ability as craftsman are mingled both with confusions about the
distinctions between craftsmanship and genius on the one hand
and, on the other, with his dominating notion that his possession of
Lucrezia, his image of perfection, somehow compensates for the
fact that he has not become one with the great. What Shakespeare
and Milton are to Keats in the rich embarrassments of the poetic
tradition,[14] Michelangelo and Rafael are to Andrea, though the lat-

ter unfortunately is totally overwhelmed by his perception of the major distinction between his art and theirs. Andrea, at the close of the poem's fifth part, has not changed, for all his interior journeying, from what he was when the poem opened. In a triumph of structural technique helping to create character, Browning has Andrea return in the poem's sixth section to the imagery and tone of the first section in a pattern similar to Blake's return in the final stanza of "The Tyger" to the "fearful symmetry" of the first, and in a manner reminiscent of the structural turning in upon itself that seems essential to the effectiveness of the Romantic meditative ode in general. The poetic structure represented by the Coleridgean "snake with its Tail in its Mouth" seems to be a product of the intensifying self-concern of the Romantic poets, a form developed indeed to express that concern. The new home it finds in the dramatic monolog, despite the masks and transformations, testifies to the continuity of the theme of self-concern and creative anxiety from the Romantics to the Victorians.

Andrea admits (ll. 198-243) that the evidence and argument for his reputation and achievement as painter are of value to him only in so far as they strengthen his case with Lucrezia. Is she pleased both with what his potential achievement was and that he has sacrificed so much for her? Is she "not grateful?" The peak of Andrea's feelings has been reached. The graph now charts a descent into the imagery and tone of the poem's first section. The wasteland images of twilight, darkness, and death are repeated in a tone of tired impotence; the plea for love and loyalty is made against an acknowledged and accepted background of infidelity; the earlier references to material corruption are amplified in the references to gold; Andrea's satisfaction in the technical sterility of his work and the solace he finds in this work is summarized; and the section ends with the final symbol for Andrea's renunciation of the search for the creative imagination and for the abdication of artistic responsibility: Lucrezia and money, one and inseparable. He must buy her minimal tolerance. The symbol of craftsmanlike perfection, when isolated from spirit, is inseparable from the basest kinds of material transactions. So complete can be the failure of the artist, so threatening are the dangers, that Browning can equate such failure with

the kind of materialistic prostitution of values and achievements
that he and his fellow Victorian "prophets" saw as the major danger to man in modern society. Andrea gives her the money she has
requested and, with never a reply from the Sphinx within, asks,
"Love, does that please you? Ah, but what does he, / The Cousin!
What does he to please you more?" [15]

The poem's final section completes the leveling off of the
hardly dynamic emotional graph of Andrea's feelings, as he briefly
summarizes a few of the details of his life against a background of
self-justifying determinism and a vision of the utopian possibility of
a second chance in heaven. That opportunity, if it came, he admits,
would result again in his failure to succeed in the competition for
greatness. Da Vinci, Rafael, Michelangelo," still they overcome /
Because there's still Lucrezia—as I choose" (ll. 264-265). Both
Browning and Andrea stress that he has chosen his own destiny as a
manifestation of character. The final admission of self-responsibil-
ity, no matter how likely we may feel that it will be followed in Andrea's "real" life by another search for a scapegoat in this pattern of
rationalization, leaves Andrea at his high point of moral stature in
the poem. But the minor heroism of acknowledgement of responsibility, even if only acknowledgment of his inability to escape the
conditions of his character or fate, is sharply undercut by the
poem's final line: "Again the Cousin's whistle! Go, my Love" (l.
266). Andrea's capitulation to that aspect of himself that Lucrezia
represents, in this emphatic position in the poem, seems to have
been achieved with hardly a struggle.

This comes as no surprise. The imagery of the poem and the
depiction of Lucrezia in particular has prepared us for this inevita-
bility. "She is one of his paintings come to life . . . a true symbol
for certain characteristics of Andrea," as Park Honan remarks.[16]
One interpretive step further suggests that she has no independent
and "realistic" existence within this poem except as a projection of
Andrea's own death impulse. She is a personification of the death
of his creativity in a bifurcation of his personality of such long
standing and of such severity that the original potential of his imagination and art are hardly visible, even in the "golden" past. Andrea
and his projections, among them Lucrezia, reinforce the structure

of emotionless rationalization with the wasteland imagery peculiar to him.

The poem is set at twilight, the very time, with its absence of light, that denies the condition needed by the painter for his creativity. The temporary darkness of Andrea's studio represents the permanent darkness of his inner light, the flame that never was, except in his desires, and the light that never will be. The absence of emotional contrasts in the poem's structure is paralleled by an absence of references to physical heat or to hot colors in the poem's imagery. The predominant "common grayness" that "silvers everything," noticed by all critics of the poem, represents the interior purgatory, the emotionless neutrality, of Andrea's life. The "autumn that grows, autumn in everything," a further development of the time-season imagery of the poem, suggests that, indeed, Andrea's life is a version of the death-in-life of "The Ancient Mariner." Andrea's essence has long ago died; grace has been withdrawn. This preternatural stillness in the poem, the absence of emotion, of the correspondent breeze, of heat, of strong color, all help to create the painterly version of the barren crags and deep crevices of traditional wasteland moonscapes. Lucrezia herself is the epitome of this moonscape, a projection of Andrea's deep commitment to sterile perfection as a value that defines his character and characterlessness: "my face, my moon, my everybody's moon."

Connected to this bright but destructive moon is the color gold that ordinarily would be used as a contrast to the colorless neutrality of Andrea's twilight. The cold, perfect, and almost colorless moon, epitomized in Lucrezia's sterile perfection, is first cousin to golden coins, "the thirteen scudi for the ruff," in an equation which equates Lucrezia and money, perfection and materialism. Even Andrea's life at the court of Francis I, usually interpreted as a time of the triumph of the creative within Andrea, represents a stage in his betrayal of his own imagination, so the imagery suggests. The monarch's look was "golden," he jingled "his gold chain in my ear," "too live the life grew, golden and not grey," and "fierce bright gold, / That gold of his I did cement them with!" Though Andrea remembers those former days as a time of opportunity and hope, Browning seems to be suggesting that even then Andrea radically misunderstood the nature of art and the relationship between materialism and creativity. Had Andrea not stolen Francis's money, a fact within the context of the poem,[17] and had Lucrezia not "grown restless" or indeed had she never existed as an historical personage, Andrea's accomplishment would have been no more than it was. He would have created another Lucrezia.

He also would have found his autumnal garden in which he could see mirrored in semi-darkness the emotionless evening. Twice Andrea uses images of cloistered restriction, of circumscribed gardens, to indicate the prison house of his soul. Andrea's world is a caged exterior representation of the prison within, similar to the oak tree in which Merlin finally imprisons himself, a variation of all those internal prisons of nineteenth-century literature in which in an act of suicidal despair the artist locks himself forever. "All living things become themselves not only by growth from the inside, but by the transformation of what surrounds them. Everything in their neighborhood must be made over in their own image. . . ."[18] Since safety and restriction are the needs of Andrea's being, they are the conditions of his landscape, perfect but safe. From his studio window he sees a "convent-wall" which "holds the trees safer, huddled more inside." "The last monk leaves" Andrea's garden. Not even the minimal emotion institutionalized in the figure of the monk, whose associations are ascetic and otherworldly, remains, suggesting that Andrea's province of emptiness and death in its excess drives out even the human figure or profession that most ordinarily would maintain the association. Later in the poem (ll. 169-170), Andrea remarks: "And I'm the weak-eyed bat no sun should tempt / Out of the grange whose four walls make his world." Here, the temptation was Francis's gold, as destructive an element as Lucrezia's perfection. The image of the restricted garden is complemented by references to other enclosures, especially by references to walls: "the convent wall," "this chamber," "whose four walls make his world," "upon a palace wall for Rome to see," "the melancholy little house," "the walls become illumined . . . fierce bright gold," "the subjects for his corridor," "this house," and finally the vision of that heavenly competition on the "four great walls in the New Jerusalem" which Andrea is destined to lose "be-

8

"Le Byron de Nos Jours"

BROWNING RARELY WRITES about writers. Painters and musicians are his delight, subject matter for more than two dozen of his monologs. Often, he uses these professions as types of the artist in general rather than as illustrations of specific craft. Indeed, this habit may be a variation of Browning's "objectifying" impulse and commitment, discussed in his essay on Shelley in which, by implication, he associates himself not with the subjective Shelley but with the objective Shakespeare.[1] John Stuart Mill's early criticism of the "morbid self-consciousness" of *Pauline* (1833) possibly bit so deep as not only to have sent Browning in search of the objective dramatic monolog form but also to have created a predilection for finding surrogates in his monologs for the writer as creative artist.[2]

However, Browning sometimes writes in his own voice, and "One Word More," published in 1855 as an epilog to Men and Women, illustrates his rare willingness to discuss himself and his craft. In "Dis Aliter Visum; or, Le Byron de Nos Jours" (1864), a neglected monolog of some complexity, Browning puts a writer, a poet "famous . . . for verse and worse," at the center of the poem. This "Byron of our day" is a failure at life and art and, consequently, deserves to be compared to "Pictor Ignotus" (1845) and "Andrea del Sarto" (1855).

The small measure of critical concern paid to "Pictor Ignotus" is quite clear in that the only significant discussion appears in a brief article refuting William DeVane's interpretation of the poem's historical context on the grounds that the poem's speaker lives in the "high," not the early Renaissance, and the poem "is an expression of personal temperament, not an illustration of the development of Italian painting in the 16th century." [3] In his 1955 revision of A Browning Handbook, DeVane admits that this argument is "persuasive," though he does not relinquish the notion that "the speaker of 'Pictor Ignotus' is a belated traditionalist who has been left stranded by the change." [4] That is almost all we hear about the poem, except for an undeveloped comparison between "Pictor Ignotus" and "Andrea del Sarto" pointing out that "it was less a Renaissance picture than a timeless study in failure, reflecting in part Browning's own ill-success in finding applause and a public." [5] As in almost all discussions of "Andrea," so too with the earlier poem; it is seen as a realistic monolog in the context of Browning's concern with personality and the theme of success and failure. But the role of the painter as representative of artists in general, and of poets in particular, needs to be stressed.[6] The poem should be viewed against the background of the general Romantic and Victorian concern with creativity, imagination, and the artist as the subject of poetry. Dim reflections of the Shelley he never was and the personal experience of years of comparative obscurity appear more often than has been recognized in the poems Browning wrote about the failure of artists.[7]

Pictor Ignotus, the unknown painter, has forfeited his stake in the competition for artistic greatness in deference to an inner voice which warned him that to mix his art with the reality of the world inevitably would undermine the commitment and the accomplishment. The short, seventy-two line monolog falls into two parts: the painter's assertion of his potential in the past to have "painted pictures like that youth's / Ye praise so" (ll. 1-2)[8] and his explanation of his purposeful choice of undistinguished artistic anonymity. Unlike Andrea's claim in a context of self-justification made more self-serving by his need to persuade Lucrezia to "sit here by the window" with her hand in his "and look a half-hour forth on Fiesole, / Both of one mind, . . . / Quietly, quietly the evening through," the unknown painter's account of his failure as artist seems sincere and acceptable. Andrea did his weak best to be a great artist and failed; Pictor Ignotus never tried. But the motivation for this abdication of effort, this rejection of "the act of the mind," seems entirely credible. In the poem's first half, the unknown painter convincingly states in vivid and concrete terms that he had indeed felt the impulse of creativity strongly.

There is no cause to suspect the painter's motives. Pictor Ignotus has no special reason to rationalize. His description of his creative impulse is so similar to Browning's typical depiction in his poetry of the true poet that there is little doubt that the painter's curiously perverse choice of career has anything to do with lack of talent. He manages to convince us that he has the potential spiritual and artistic dynamism that Andrea so clearly lacks. In fact, he describes a protean potentiality that combines both the characteristics of the subjective and the objective poet discussed by Browning in his 1852 essay on Shelley. The objective poet "is properly the *poietes*, the fashioner; and the things fashioned, his poetry, will of necessity be substantive, projected from himself and distinct." [9] The subjective poet, "gifted like the objective poet with the fuller perception of nature and man, is impelled to embody the thing he perceives, not so much with reference to the many below as to the One above him, the supreme Intelligence which apprehends all things in their absolute truth—an ultimate view ever aspired to, if but partially attained, by the poet's own soul." The monologist of "Pictor Ignotus" says:

> *Never did fate forbid me, star by star,*
> *To outburst on your night with all my gift*
> *   Of fires from God: nor would my flesh have shrunk*
> *From seconding my soul, with eyes uplift*
> *   And wide to heaven, or, straight like thunder, sunk*
> *To the centre, of an instant. . . .*
>
> (ll. 4-9)

Clearly, Browning is describing the subjective artist in terms similar to those he was to use in his essay of 1852, just as it is evident that in the following lines Browning's unknown painter is describing the objective poet as well:

> *   or around*
> *   Turned calmly and inquisitive, to scan*
> *The license and the limit, space and bound,*
> *   Allowed to truth made visible in man.*
> *And, like that youth ye praise so, all I saw,*
> *   Over the canvas could my hand have flung,*
> *Each face obedient to its passion's law. . . .*
>
> (ll. 9-15)

Unlike Andrea, he has no taint of materialism or commercialism. The unknown painter has not been tempted by sterile perfection or gold. There is a passage on this point in the essay on Shelley so closely describing Andrea that it suggests both the poem and the essay were closely connected in Browning's mind:

> The love of displaying power for the display's sake, the love of riches, of distinction, of notoriety,—the desire of a triumph over rivals, and the vanity in the applause of friends,—each and all of such whetted appetites grown intenser by exercise and increasingly sagacious as to the best and readiest means of self-appeasement,—while for any of their ends, whether the money or the pointed finger of the crowd, or the flattery and hate to heart's content, there are cheaper prices to pay, they will all find soon enough, than a bestowment of a life upon a labour, hard, slow, and not sure.[10]

The unknown painter has not succumbed to any of these corrupting temptations. His dilemma is more intense, personal, and relevant to Browning's own career, though his solution denies the validity of making the parallel a complete one. It is as if the dilemma in which Browning shows the unknown painter is one which he himself confronted after the crushing disappointment of the criticism of his early "subjective" works, later obliquely described in his essay on Shelley. Like Browning himself, the unknown painter has the capacity to be either subjective lyric poet or objective dramatic poet. Unlike Browning, he chooses neither, and turns to the safety of complete withdrawal from artistic competition. He is Browning's extreme representation of the artist who purposefully has renounced success in both the lyric and dramatic modes because of the difficulty of sustaining his equilibrium against society's hypothetical criticism of his specific paintings and the world's attitude toward art in general.[11]

The imagined fame that seems so sweet in the painter's projection has its negative side. If the poet's powers are limitlessly extensive and heroically combine both the lyric and the objective mode, the success that he imagines must result from the exhibition of such powers. Inherent within this power, however, is a frightening disregard for the extreme sensitivity of the great artist and for the independent integrity of his art products. The unknown artist is both frightened and repelled by the prospect of the results of such success; while his talents are heroic his courage is certainly less than that. Here the portrait has similarities with Andrea's. Though the unknown painter's potential is much greater, they both fail to achieve basically through a failure of character rather than of art. Whereas Andrea is without emotion and sensitivity, without feeling and will, the unknown painter fails because of an excess of sensitivity and emotion. Indeed, he has the supreme will to renounce, as an existential act, what Browning suggests is an immense creative capability. The extent of the painter's hypersensitivity is suggested by the comparison of the relationship between himself and his possible public to that of a nun shrinking from a soldier (ll. 47-48), and by his brilliant animation of his paintings which, like people, must suffer indignities from their purchasers:

> *And where they live needs must our pictures live*
> *And see their faces, listen to their prate,*
> *Partakers of their daily pettiness,*
> *Discussed of—"This I love, or this I hate,*
> *This likes me more, and this affects me less!"*
> (ll. 52-56)

The imagined reaction of the world to his art is depicted by the unknown painter as if his choice had been to be a subjective or lyric painter and had been judged as such. Certainly the painter's vision of extraordinary fame is an imaginative projection on Browning's part in 1845, not at all uncongenial to the neglected poet who would have liked "to live, I and my picture, linked / With love about, and praise" (ll. 26-27). Probably "those cold faces that begun / To press on me and judge me" (ll. 46-47) echo in some way Browning's painful experience with Mill, whose contemporaries, by the way, often enough used that same adjective "cold" to describe his appearance.[12] The retreat from the confrontation with self and society is one that Browning's nineteenth-century predecessors would have well understood and appreciated. In their own ways, Coleridge, Keats, and Tennyson express the same anxieties in both lyric and dramatic form.

Ultimately the nineteenth-century concern, more intense as the century advanced, with the corruption of art and with the gradual intensification of a materialistic atmosphere hostile to its flourishing dominates "Pictor Ignotus," as it does so much of Browning's, Tennyson's, and Arnold's poetry. The unknown painter solaces himself for the occasional depression resulting from the monotony of his activity by proclaiming that "at least no merchant traffics in my heart" (l. 62), as one does, of course, in Andrea's. If this is rationalization for timidity and cowardice, it compares suggestively with an attitude that Browning often expressed when defending his reliance upon his father's economic support.[13] This kind of anti-materialism is so common in nineteenth-century literature and culture that it needs no biographical relevance. In the end, the unknown painter renounces, and by doing so cuts rather emphatically the biographical umbilical cord, the necessary mixture of good and evil, of pure and impure, that Browning believed in:[14]

> *Blown harshly, keeps the trump its golden cry?*
> *Tastes sweet the water with such specks of earth?*
> (ll. 71-72)

Structurally, "Pictor Ignotus" is a tightly unified monolog in which the dialectical relationship between the painter's past and present exists on the level of simple comparison. In this sense, the poem has a directness of technique, diction, and structure that is unusual in Browning's monologs about art and artists. The poem has a lyrical directness, uncomplicated by the degrees and levels of distancing between himself and the character in which Browning as dramatic monologist specialized. This is not the case in "Dis Aliter Visum; or Le Byron de Nos Jours" (1864), one of Browning's most complicated and ironic dramatic monologs, a poem in which Browning not only deals with the failed artist in general but with the failed poet. In the ironic "Byron of our Day," Browning carries forward his own and his century's concern with the relationship between character and artistic success and provides a fascinating variation of the artist in wasteland, whose vision of the nature of art and artistic success completely denies the powers of the imagination in which the Romantics had so wanted to believe.

Divided into thirty stanzas of five lines each, "Dis Aliter Visum," translated as "the gods willed it otherwise," presents the words of "a woman of about thirty" who addresses her former prospective husband, "a famous French poet whom she had last seen ten years before" at the same seaside resort in Brittany.[15] Stanza I informs us that it is evening. We can assume that it is summer since there are references later to flowers and the hot sun. Thus, it is established that the speaker is not a timid girl, but a mature woman, whose conversation is frank, and whose relationship with the man she addresses has been interrupted by a decade of separation. Then, they were almost lovers; now, they "meet this evening, friends or what?" In stanzas II-V our speaker imagines in direct dialog form, in the words that she puts into the mind or mouth of the poet ten years ago, the poet's condescending sympathy with her naive enthusiasm for art and learning. With an occasional reference to the landscape to set the scene(VI-VII), she imagines, with some regret, what words he would have used to persuade himself to overcome his scruples and marry her (VIII-XIII). Her imagined words become a dramatic monolog. She becomes a creator herself, using language to shape her version of the poet, whom she postulates would think of their marriage as a January-May relationship. Her vision of his character is an incisive one, as she projects in him a rather stolid appreciation of her virtues, combining both youth and physical beauty, both wealth, "money in the three percents," and a deeply respectful appreciation of the wisdom of her choice. She says that he thought her choice of him would "seem profound," suggesting that he believes her willingness to marry him was partly based on the need to satisfy her ego which, of course, reveals his own to be grotesquely immense. The complications of this handling of complex time sequences and verbal projections become even more involved when, in stanzas XV-XX, the speaker not only imagines what the poet would have thought and said, but imagines what she would have thought and said in response. The dramatic monolog form, the direct presentation of a character's words, has become a structure "like a set of Chinese boxes," [16] encapsulating a number of speeches which in turn are dramatic monologs in the mind of the original speaker.

In her mind she reconstructs what she believes the poet had thought when he had concluded that their marriage could not be, that "an hour's perfection can't recur." She answers in her thoughts what she imagines the poet was thinking, remembering the moment in which the decision to separate had been translated into physical communication. Then

> It was, no doubt, you ceased that least
> Light pressure of my arm in yours.
>
> (ll. 87-88)

So she thinks she remembers. She has projected his thoughts into the future of their relationship, his reaction to their possible mar-

turned out otherwise. We can grant her that psychological weakness, and credit Browning's insight. What is somewhat miraculous, however, is that this is all an internal drama, and the poet has at the most a very tenuous realistic existence. He is never quoted directly; he is not described physically in terms that can be credited to his or to a third party's voice. Everything we know of him we learn from the speaker. Like a puppet master pulling the strings of her own creation against a manipulated background, she creates not only his words and his thoughts but everything he is. This suggests that she is playing a rhetorical and psychological game in which the expectations of the past are being used as a weapon in the present to lament not four dull lives, not even two, but mainly her own. One has the impression that the poet hardly listens. That this graceful, subtle woman who can spin such enchanting webs of language and point of view resorts a number of times to blunt and angry direct address, such as, "Stop, let me have the truth of that"; "now I may speak: you fool, for all / Your lore," reinforces the notion that his mind is still on "the Fortieth spare Arm-chair," or on "Stephanie" who "sprained last night her wrist," or some other irrelevant detail.

Not only her point of view and rhetoric but her imagery pronounces disrespectful judgment on the poet, revealing him to be a tedious bore both a decade ago as well as now. We see the enthusiastic young girl of twenty and the poet through the eyes of a mature woman who clearly values her former naiveté more highly than his former and present knowing self-protectiveness. Consequently, her imagery is particularly instructive. She remarks in the first stanza that then they had met in the morning; now they meet in the evening, suggesting, no matter how offhandedly mentioned, the repeated symbolic emphasis on twilight in "Andrea del Sarto." Her first speech in stanza II refers to the molten and energetic sea, "a Mass of brass / That sea looks, blazing underneath," suggesting that the double level of activity and feeling that the sea manifests relates to her own consciousness then.[17] Confidence in the future underlies her remark that "while up the cliff-road edged with heath, / We took the turns nor came to harm." In stanzas III-V, the first projected words of the poet, the imagery changes, anticipating the abrupt transformation of mood in stanza VI. The speaker asks what would have happened if he had determined to have her, while at the same time she describes a change in the landscape from molten sea of energy and cliff-road of expectation to the church that promises not marriage but separation:

> And did you, when we faced the church
> With spire and sad slate roof, aloof
> From human fellowship so far,
> Where a few graveyard crosses are,
> And garlands for the swallows' perch. . . .
>
> (stanza VI)

She patterns his mental twists as he argues himself out of the wisdom of such a proposal in imagery which moves from the cliff and the sea, past the churchyard and the graves, down to the sand and the baths ("feet, feelings must descend the hill") and, finally, to the triviality, the corruption, of "love-freaks" (XII) and "three percents" (XIII). Her words in stanza XX reinforce her association with water, heights, and flowers, for the poet is made to imagine that he would be unhappy in exchanging his poetic accomplishments for "two cheeks freshened by youth and sea . . . all for a nosegay . . . fields on flowers, untried each side." It is quite clear that she might wonder now why she had wanted to marry him at all. Unlike the Amy of "Locksley Hall," she is not the betrayer but the betrayed. Browning's poet has completely deserted the field of action for which Tennyson's speaker is searching.

The accomplishments of this poet are meagre. Though he may be "famous . . . for verse and worse," possibly an occasional excursion into critical prose, like an introductory essay on Shelley, and sure of "the Fortieth spare Arm-chair" in the French Academy, there is no evaluative mention of his poetic accomplishments. While it is true, as is not the case with the unknown painter or with Andrea del Sarto, that this poet is being judged by the speaker as a human being rather than as an artist, Browning frequently warns against such a distinction and insists upon the necessary relationship between ethics and character on the one hand and artistic achievement on the other. In stanza XIX, the poet has made it clear that the basis of his rejection of their potential relationship was his decision that there could be no coexistence between his artistic needs and his marriage to her. But, for some unexplained reason, he has found his dedication to his craft compatible with his marriage to the dancer Stephanie. To her credit, the speaker restricts herself to a catty remark about the vileness of his wife's dancing and does not attempt to suggest the grounds for their greater compatibility. The poem suggests, however, that the poet responded more favorably to marriage with a professional artist than to an amateur enthusiast. Browning himself, of course, married a professional artist with results that he seems never to have regretted, though in the opinion of the speaker the poet's marriage to Stephanie has been a failure just as in her dancing "her vogue has had its day" (XXX).

Having judged that the negative decision had been made, the speaker concludes: "That ended me." She summarizes the imagery of the preceding stanza in a matter-of-fact tone that catches both the dryness of the poet's personality and the undercurrent of deep feeling implicit in her stoic acceptance of their separation, feeling basically so deep that ten years later, having had the chance to evaluate what had happened, she expresses it in the bitter words of stanza XXIII: "That ended me." She says earlier:

> You judged the porch
> We left by, Norman; took our look
> At sea and sky; wondered so few
> Find out the place for air and view;
> Remarked the sun began to scorch;
>
> Descended, soon regained the baths,
> And then, good-by!
> (stanzas XXI-XXII)

In her view of the poet, irrelevant architecture takes precedent over human feeling. At best he is a visitor to the landscape with which she has been associated. There is no sympathy between natural sunlight and this unnatural man. The descent to the "baths" carries the movement of imagery from highland to sea level, associating their separation not with the untamed sea but with the domesticated "baths." Immediately, the change in physical landscape finds its temporal parallel. In stanza XXII, we learn that the similar but changed setting of the natural environment of their earlier meeting has been replaced by tedious artificiality:

> *Ten years! We meet: you tell me, now,*
> *By a window-seat for that cliff-brow,*
> *On carpet-stripes for those sand-paths.*

Her address to the poet in the present (stanzas XXIII-XXIX) begins on a note of abuse ("you fool") and concludes with an image of a "mere star-fish" that summarizes the imagery of the preceding stanzas and epitomizes Browning's well-known emphasis on success as a striving towards unreachable goals, mainly the unification of the total personality.

Sounding much like the familiar surrogate for Browning in his poetry, our speaker asks her Byron a series of rhetorical questions, all of which make clear that he has missed "success" by embracing success, that man's field of action is the earth, that the time for bold action is always the present, and that love is an ultimate value that must be translated into actions that validate it.[18] The questions are posed in the negative, reflecting the normally negative characteristics of the poet's thought and life. In stanza XXVII, she puts the seal of condemnation on his philosophy: "This you call wisdom?" In stanza XXVIII, she introduces the image of the "star-fish":

> *Let the mere star-fish in his vault*
> *Crawl in a wash of weed, indeed,*
> *Rose-jacynth to the finger-tips:*
> *He, whole in body and soul, outstrips*
> *Man, found with either in default.*

The tedium of the atmosphere of the entire poem and the poet's triviality are captured in the image of the star-fish which combines both something lofty and heavenly with something primitive and scuttling to represent the impulse towards sterile perfection that has always motivated the poet. This is a familiar theme in Browning, but one of its most exciting representations. That star-fish, we are told, a creature which crawls in weeds, is not only monochrome but is "whole in body and soul." Certainly this poet is more like Prufrock than Byron, even to the association with underwater imagery and a trivial marine creature. The star-fish, indeed, has reached the limit of its growth, its perfection, just as the poet has reached the limit of his. Such expansions in the Browning lexicon are contractions, as if the meagerness of one's sense of self can create a self with too narrow boundaries. The anxieties of the traditional Romantic poet concerning his creativity have been minimized by this poet, but at the cost of an almost unconscious renunciation of the possibilities of growth. These limitations are like safe boundaries out of which the self will not dare to step; hence the complacent smugness of the poet or painter who feels totally master of his small domain and craft, like Andrea within the framework of his paintings and the enclosures of his sequestered garden. The perfection of the star-fish, like the enclosed manageable world of the poet, is a metaphor for the prison-house of the self, for the oak tree in which Merlin has imprisoned himself, for the innumerable voluntary prisons of the self into which nineteenth-century poets are tempted to secure themselves forever, freed from the burden of creativity and lost to "use and name and fame." This impulse towards self-containment, towards delimiting the structural and skeletal possibilities of one's soul, especially on the narrow scale suggested by the star-fish, is life-destructive:

> But what's whole, can increase no more,
>   Is dwarfed and dies, since here's its sphere.
> The devil laughed at you in his sleeve!
>   (stanza XXIX)

"Dis Aliter Visum" is a perplexing but typical Browning monolog whose complex manipulations of point of view within point of view do not in the end obscure the fact that not only does the theme of the poem run through many Browning poems but that the poet, the "Byron of his day," like Andrea del Sarto, is one among many versions in Browning of the failed artist. The title itself is a puzzle. Houghton and Stange translate Virgil's words as "the Gods willed it otherwise"; DeVane translates it as "to the gods it seemed otherwise." [19] The former translation is preferable for it contains the ironic note that Browning includes in the subtitle. The phrase suggests Arnold's ironic and calmly despairing words in "To Marguerite—Continued": "A God, a God, their severance ruled! / And bade betwixt their shores to be / The unplumb'd, salt, estranging sea." [20] Similarly, in Browning's poem responsibility cannot be shifted to the shoulders of a deific scapegoat. But whereas Arnold blames not himself but some unknown agency, possibly fate, for this world he never made, Browning or at least his poem's speaker blames this poet for the destruction of four souls. There is ample evidence that Browning as relativist appreciated the idea that character is destiny, without ever forsaking the existential premise that every individual plays some important role in "forging" his character. This artist, then, has made himself and his destiny. Browning has made him a peculiarly Browningesque representative of the potential Romantic artist who has deserted his calling, or disregarded it, and lost not only his art but his soul. His is not a failure but a rejection of imagination and Romantic creativity. As poet, the "Byron of our Day's" sense of self is a demeaned and constricted one, depicted so brilliantly that one cannot help but speculate that Browning's own sense of self was astonishingly complex and potentially fallen.

9

The Banquet of the Muses

ARNOLD'S "EMPEDOCLES ON ETNA" is the most sustained poem to come out of the growing mid-nineteenth century realization of the unsuitability of the Romantic vision of the poet and the creative process to Victorian aspirations for life and art. Significantly, the poem's structure and imagery take this theme as subject. In it, Arnold struggles to cast off the brilliant but somewhat burdensome Romantic heritage, which had been lightened only slightly by the local and topographical successes of "Wordsworth's healing power," [1] the poet who taught John Stuart Mill "what would be the perennial sources of happiness when all the greater evils of life shall have been removed." [2] These evils, in Arnold's eyes, had increased and intensified. Thus, the poet among the early Romantics

124

who shows the most similarities to Arnold's characteristic tensions, structures, and images is not Wordsworth but Coleridge. In "Empedocles on Etna," Arnold is intent on dramatizing, in a form and with imagery inherited from the Romantic past, the inappropriateness of such structure and imagery to the problems of the mid-nineteenth century.[3] At the same time, he is suggesting a general view of man and a specific view of the poet which promises a new vocabulary for a new age. Revelation will become epiphany, the mind turned in upon itself will become the "act of the mind" in search of the poem. Certainly "Empedocles" is a far less despairing poem than critics have thought. A recent scholar is quite apt in noting that "when we charge Arnold with losing the Romantic faith, we must remember that this faith had already been lost by the very men who created it."[4]

Though he seems to have had the least influence on Arnold,[5] Coleridge's bifurcation into thinker and poet provides an important parallel with Arnold's into Empedocles and Callicles. Despite the conventions of the dramatic form, "Empedocles on Etna" is a pseudodramatic poem in the Romantic tradition. The obvious absence of action and plot, which Arnold somewhat disingenuously bewailed, is completely consistent with its allegorical cast. While one aspect of the poem looks outward toward an assessment of the Romantic tradition, another looks inward to the poet's divided self, a conventional Romantic exploration, in an internal drama in which Callicles and Empedocles represent opposing forces within Arnold's own imagination. That Arnold in his famous renunciatory preface of 1853 should apply Aristotelian standards of action and catharsis to his poem reveals how far he had moved intellectually from the tradition of "Hyperion," "Christabel," and even *The Prelude*. Like Coleridge after 1802, Arnold after 1855 subordinated his poetic "ministry" to a larger commitment to a philosophical religion whose boundaries were not to be the depths of the imagination but the heights of heaven—the mind was to make a synthesis for which the imagination had shown the need.[6]

In a rather unusual approach, Arnold wrote a poem concerning this change in ministries before the alteration had occurred and indeed while the turmoil was in process. This accounts for some of the poem's ambiguities and the subsequent disagreements about which character represents Arnold, some critics giving the honor to the joyless Stoic philosopher, others to the young harp player.[7] This also explains some of the poem's structural and imagistic peculiarities. Arnold is using structure and imagery to help create a tone which his poem in theme attempts to reject. Perhaps this is why not many readers have been convinced of the wisdom, and even the emotional sincerity, of Arnold's choice.[8] To reject the kind of poetry "Empedocles on Etna" represents means to reject the only kind of poetry of which Arnold was capable. One of our best critics has remarked that the answer to Arnold's dilemma "lay in the cruel effort and continued self-expenditure of a series of Empedoclean victories, not in the carefully qualified betrayal, the compromise of life and art . . . which his Mask as Critic represents." But, like Coleridge, Arnold compromised to "save his soul." [9] Anticipations of the compromise appear in much of Arnold's early poetry. The great strength of "Empedocles on Etna" is that it effectively dramatizes a predecision stage of insecure and divided loyalties in his movement toward "the city of God."

The conflict between these forces in Arnold's personality early in the 1850s is emphasized in the contrast between the cool mythic inviolability of the Romantic harpist and the resigned melancholy dejection of the philosopher. Throughout the poem, the relationship is one of student to master, son to father, and, ultimately, of one aspect of the self to another aspect of the self.[10] All of the poem's references to and evaluations of the Romantic tradition involve not a rejection of that heritage but a comparison between the Romantic poet who has succeeded and the Romantic poet who has failed.[11] Yet, Empedocles' plunge into the volcano makes it quite clear that there shall be no easy solution to the deep depression and inactivity of the failed poet who has reached a state of paralysis far more intense than that depicted by any previous Romantic poet, except perhaps Coleridge in "Dejection: An Ode" and Keats in "Ode to a Nightingale." The volcano may promise purgation and rebirth, but the myth of metempsychosis, connected normally to an anti-Arnoldian and anti-Tennysonian "cycle of Cathay" rather than to culture or creativity, hardly suggests that Empedocles will be reborn as Callicles, as the poet he once almost was. What is this fatal illness of the spirit from which Empedocles suffers? Why, in the context of the poem, has he climbed to the dangerous and barren height of pure fire?

The poem provides a number of answers, some rather deceiving because this is a dramatic poem and the credibility of what characters say must be carefully evaluated. Pausanias is the first interpreter of Empedocles' illness, seeing it mainly in terms of social context, the change between the conditions of Empedocles' field of action in the past and the present. The times, clearly, are at fault. The charismatic powers of Empedocles, connected to his mastery of music, have been paralyzed, the direct result not of interior forces but of exterior, social degeneration:

> *but now, since all*
> *Clouds and grows daily worse in Sicily,*
> *Since broils tear us in twain, since this new swarm*
> *Of sophists has got empire in our schools*
> *Where he was paramount, since he is banish'd*
> *And lives a lonely man in triple gloom—*
> *He grasps the very reins of life and death.*
>
> (act 1, sc. 1, 119-125)

Empedocles has been driven to the point of suicide by social and intellectual ostracism, Pausanius argues, and, in response to Callicles' amazement that he has been able to escort Empedocles in his present "man-hating mood," reveals that he seeks to discover from Empedocles the secret of his power, that his motives are exploitative in a tainted student-teacher relationship. Pausanias wants to know "what might profit me; / That is, the secret of this miracle." Callicles' answer is brief, just as Empedocles' explanation is to be long. He denies Pausanias' account: the fault is not in our stars but in ourselves, and

> *There is some root of suffering in himself,*
> *Some secret and unfollow'd vein of woe,*
> *Which makes the time look black and sad to him.*
>
> (act 1, sc. 1, 151-153)

All that Empedocles says in his long, didactic speech in act 1, scene 2, confirms this explanation. Nothing that he says in act 2 effectively denies that he is the cause of his own suffering.

Empedocles reveals no secret that Pausanias wants to hear, making the central, long section of the poem one of Arnold's most subtle exercises in providing contrast between the surface language and advice of a character and his more deeply held contrary feelings. Pausanias, the non-poet of the poem, the false-physician whose powers are undermined by superstition and wishful thinking, who desires Empedocles to explain to him the origin and control of true magic, provokes Empedocles to lecture at self-defeating length on the need to reject myth and expectation. The answer to Pausanias' request comes in the language of Stoic philosophy, some of which Arnold undoubtedly inherited from his sources for the poem,[12] much of which, however, seems a deliberate attempt by Arnold to emphasize not only the absurdity of Pausanias' exterior search for what must be sought within, but to call attention to the tremendous gap between Empedocles' "buried life" and his surface life. Empedocles expounds at tedious length in a diction and a verse form that can suggest only pretentious sterility to emphasize a philosophy the very reverse of the one he acts out. Like a teacher who presents his life as a model of how not to live, Empedocles presents a philosophy directly opposed to the condition of joy that he has always sought, and the lack of which drives him to an ambiguous suicide.

Commentators have remarked on the connection between Arnold's frequent use of the word *joy* and its use also by Wordsworth and Coleridge. Certainly the nature of Empedocles' illness is no mystery to the reader of Romantic poetry from Blake to Byron. Two traditions predominate. In the minor one, melancholy, depression, and eventual paralysis result from the poet's awareness of the "worry, the fever, and the fret" that inevitably occur when he realizes that he lives in a corrupt world of mutability. In the major one, perhaps conditioned by his awareness of exterior corruption and mutability, often against a background of deep epistemological incertitude about the nature of reality, the poet confronts a crisis of confidence not only in the general value of socially organized life but in the cosmic purpose that he believed had been superrationally and somewhat ineffably struggling to be revealed in his own imagination and in his own poetic language. Sometimes the doubt in this general cosmic purpose precedes loss of faith in his own ministry, sometimes the process is reversed; often the complex subtleties of such thoughts and expressions do not permit the poet or his readers to make the distinction at all. The result, however, is usually the same: negative creativity and deadness of feeling dominate, denying the value of life; and the poet's powers of emotional magnification are now enslaved to depression and paralysis. One of the most frequently considered cures is self-extinction; and, among Arnold's predecessors, Coleridge and Keats made major poetry out of the extreme solution to the predicament. Empedocles suffers from a severe form of the illness. Like a good number of nineteenth-century poets and characters within poems, he desperately seeks his "correspondent breeze," his storm, his field of action. "Ah, boil up, ye vapours! / Leap and roar, thou sea of fire," he cries, hoping to find his renewal in the seething volcano, which holds the possibility of revived joy.

In a sense, Empedocles is a fictional expression of the historical, limited Romantic poet, and Callicles represents the mythic, ideal Romantic poet. Arnold tells us that the former is insufficient unto himself, while the latter is a permanent model of the imagination who, like Wallace Stevens's "figure of capable imagination," must play

> *A tune beyond us, yet ourselves,*
> *A tune upon the blue guitar*
> *Of things exactly as they are.*

In his better days, Empedocles was a musician who played melodies upon an imaginary harp, ministering to the unseen but strongly felt:

> *He could stay swift diseases in old days*
> *Chain madmen by the music of his lyre,*

Cleanse to sweet airs the breath of poisonous streams,
And in the mountain-chinks inter the wind.
(act 1, sc. 1, 115-118)

The power of his art proved so immense that once, like the Biblical David, he could cure the diseases of the mind and body with his music.

But the physician can no longer heal himself. The positions have become reversed. The young David has become the old Saul, the young Callicles has become Empedocles, and the poet has become the philosopher whose power over other men and over the forces of nature has declined. He who formerly exerted a supreme civilizing force, chaining "madmen" with his music, has now become a social exile who neither can nor wants to use his music in the service of society. From Pausanias we learn that he has been banished, from Empedocles that he would not return for any reason. Conditions in himself and in society once permitted him a dominance over the forces of nature and a Wordsworthian movement between the city and the country, between society and solitude, which, in the present, must be rejected. We are told that formerly he was a kind of mediator between man and nature, with the power to exorcise with his music man's tainted use of natural forces, mitigating and making acceptable before the larger world of nature and the cosmos man's minor corruptions. Traditional mountain-wind imagery, like the "wind . . . Mad Lutanist" and "storm" that may "be but a mountain-birth" of Coleridge's "Dejection: An Ode," emphasizes that Empedocles' powers were so great that just as huge "mountain-chinks inter the wind," so too this magnificent artist controlled the powerful and potentially wild, even destructive, energies of creativity. Yet, so deep now is the melancholy, the depression, the joylessness within Empedocles that he renounces almost all connection with his former powers.

Empedocles had been Apollo's representative. Despite Pausanias' stress on his philosophic and political credentials, Empedocles himself emphasizes that his entire life has been devoted to the service of the Olympian god of art, whom Callicles tells us, in the last song of the poem, is completely out of his habitat on the peak of Etna: "Not here, O Apollo! Are haunts meet for thee. / But, where Helicon breaks down / In cliff to the sea," just as Empedocles the poet is below in the valley of the past.[13] For reasons best explained in terms of general Romantic melancholy and loss of creativity, Empedocles admits that he is "weary" of the "laurel bough":

> *Scornful Apollo's ensign, lie thou there!*
> *Though thou hast been my shade in the world's heat—*
> *Though I have loved thee, lived in honouring thee—*
> *Yet lie thou there*
> *My laurel bough!*
>
> (act 2, 193-197)

The dedication to art that has given his life sustenance and meaning has been infected by some Blakean "invisible worm" which has found out the poetic "bed of crimson joy"; by some Baudelairean ennui and paralysis of creative energy; by a complete loss of "the passion and the life, whose fountains are within." [14] Empedocles' vocabulary makes it clear that his is an explicit rejection of the meaningfulness, of the life-sustaining values, of the emotions and of the poems that the Romantic tradition had produced. He is weary of the solitude that the Romantics thought a precondition of the creative act; he is weary of the sublime, mythological-psychological landscape of the Romantic poet's emotions, "the black drizzling crags" of Book VI of *The Prelude*, "the rocks that muttered close upon our ear," the "deep romantic chasm" of "Kubla Khan," "the moonlit peaks" that appear frequently in Wordsworth and Coleridge, "those caves" of "Kubla Khan" and "La Belle Dame Sans Merci":

> *I am weary of thee.*
> *I am weary of the solitude*
> *Where he who bears thee must abide—*
> *Of the rocks of Parnassus,*
> *Of the gorge of Delphi,*
> *Of the moonlit peaks, and the caves.*
>
> (act 2, 198-203)

The limitations of the Romantic tradition, its unsuitability to the present condition of Empedocles, who sees it in terms not of the ideal but the real, the solitude and suffering of Coleridge and Keats, for example, in comparison to the calm invincibility of Callicles, are emphasized in a rejection of some of the major images of its great poets. The price that must be paid to make oneself a poet in this tradition is too severe. Standing guard over the Romantic landscape is Apollo, whose harsh, implacable severity has been emphasized even by Callicles, who, in the song immediately preceding this section of Empedocles' speech, has told the story of the poetic competition between Marsyas and Apollo which concludes with Apollo scornfully and unpiteously accepting his victory. Apollo's landscape and domain are fertilized by suffering and death, so high are the stakes and so ruthless the emotional forces at work:

> *Thou guardest them, Apollo!*
> *Over the grave of the slain Pytho,*
> *Though young, intolerably severe!*
> *Thou keepest aloof the profane,*
> *But the solitude oppresses thy votary!*
>   (act 2, 204-208)

Finally and emphatically it is the solitude, the sense of muteness and inarticulate separation, that defeats Empedocles because he cannot give them creative voice. He has no reservoir of joy and energy from which to water his loneliness. He has solitude without the Romantic commitment to make solitude a virtue. Callicles moves back and forth between man's society and nature's loveliness, using solitude as stimulant for his imagination which has the power through language to mediate between these worlds. Empedocles finds both worlds torturous, for he no longer has either the imagination or the language to find one or the other acceptable, and no commitment that will permit him to mediate between them. Unlike the archetypal Wordsworthian poet who sees his life as a series of movements between city and country, present and past, fact and fancy, society and solitude, in which both states are

satisfactory only because of their necessary relationship to one another, the failed Empedoclean poet finds both society and solitude
unbearable. The traditional movement no longer provides renewal
and calm; it dizzies and distresses:

> *Where shall thy votary fly then? back to men?—*
> . . . .
> *And he will fly to solitude again,*
> *And he will find its air too keen for him,*
> *And so change back; and many thousand times*
> *Be miserably bandied to and fro*
> *Like a sea-wave, betwixt the word and thee,*
> *Thou young, implacable God! and only death*
> *Can cut his oscillations short. . . .*
>   (act 2, 220-233)

Thus, the plunge into the volcano is not nearly the completely
negative act that some have suggested. Though it has elements of
ambiguity, it certainly is the most positive action taken by Empedocles in the poem. As Wordsworth drew upon the myth of prebirth in his Immortality Ode metaphorically to describe states of
the psyche, Arnold has Empedocles use the myth of metempsychosis to suggest the possibility of peace and joy in some distant future.
Perhaps Arnold would have been wiser to choose some other myth,
because the suicidal Romanticism of Empedocles' joylessness has
moved the ex-poet considerably away from the Greek legend of his
life. He seems to have more in common with the suffering, numbed
voices of "Ode to a Nightingale" and "Dejection: An Ode" than
with the classical philosopher. So the discussion of rebirth jars
somewhat and tends to confuse the meaning of the suicide. Possibly Arnold himself was fundamentally ambiguous about its significance, and the atypical Arnoldian orientalizing provided
cover.[15] Yet the volcano itself has solidity and meaning as a symbol,
even within the Romantic heritage. For Arnold frequently uses imagery from this tradition to denounce its source. The volcano is

first cousin to Coleridge's "mighty fountain" which rises out of "that deep romantic chasm,"

> Amid whose swift half-intermitted burst
> Huge fragments vaulted like rebounding hail,
> Or chaffy grain beneath the thresher's flail:
> And 'mid these dancing rocks at once and ever
> It flung up momently the sacred river.[16]

Both are origins of energy, of force, erupting mysteriously with primal creativity, and both are sources of some intense liquid:

> —Ah, boil up, ye vapours!
> Leap and roar, thou sea of fire!
> My soul glows to meet you.
> (act 2, 410-412)

The plunge into the volcano is the plunge into the mystery of the "romantic chasm," "the sacred river," the "fountain light of all our day," the burning bush, the source of energy which is "eternal delight," the confrontation of those ambiguously awesome images of both destructive and creative force embodied by Blake in the "fearful symmetry" of his tiger. For Empedocles, the leap is an attempt to find joy and energy again, or, at least, peace. The one act that builds on despair yet offers some promise of joy, fortunately, is the one act of which Empedocles is capable.

Callicles is most vividly revealed in the positioning and the substance of his five interpolated songs.[17] In counterpoint to the joyless failed poet who has lost not only his sense of emotional proportion but his sense of the beauty of language and the necessity for structured expression, Callicles represents the ideal poet whose sense of the relationship between structure and language is perfect. Empedocles is often harsh, unmelodic, and tedious. Callicles, in his dialogue with Pausanias in act 1, scene 1, combines sharpness of expression with directness of discourse; and, while Empedocles' major speech in the drama is graceless and tediously long, as if Arnold could not risk our not associating Empedocles' general breakdown with a breakdown in his language, Callicles' contribution is broken into five parts, each of which draws upon the resources of language, music, and myth. Yet the songs are not interpolated in any negative sense. Each is immediately relevant to the dramatic situation into which its sounds flow. Each contains not only a mood contrasting with or complementary to the context, but a mythical story which is direct comment on the dramatic situation of the poem. Significantly, not once does Empedocles see Callicles. Songs are always "from below," totally auditory experiences in which the independence of the sounds suggests that they come from some other than human source,[18] from the secret voice of the "deep-buried self" or from some dream-vision "damsel with a dulcimer."

Callicles' connection with nature, his constant movement between city and country, society and privacy, his student-teacher, subject-king relationship with Empedocles, his belief that Empedocles' suffering is self-inflicted, his hope to play David to Empedocles' Saul, his contempt for Pausanias' ignoble self-interest, and, finally, his great artistry are established in the short first scene of the first act. The long second scene, after a brief discussion in which Pausanias explains to Empedocles that the music they hear comes from the "sweetest harp-player in Catana" and in which Empedocles emphasizes that man can control his own destiny through his mind, contains two songs by Callicles. Between them, as if encircled, appears Empedocles' long disquisition in which he recommends to Pausanias a severe Stoic philosophy. Finally, the act concludes with Empedocles' abrupt dismissal of Pausanias in which he makes clear his resolution to return "in the sure revolutions of the world." Like Tennyson's Ulysses, an echo of which Arnold himself might have been aware, Empedocles concludes:

> *I have seen many cities in my time,*
> *Till my eyes ache with the long spectacle,*
> *And I shall doubtless see them all again.*[19]

Callicles' first song in scene 2, divided into two parts, initially proclaims the special beauty of the valley of Etna, the lower slopes of the mountain, in order to contrast the "high, well-watered dells" and "verdant sides" with "Etna beyond, in the broad glare / Of the hot noon, without a shade." This, of course, is essentially, in topographical terms, the contrast between Callicles and Empedocles, just as the second section of the song in its presentation of the myth of the "aged Centaur" and "the young Achilles" more directly presents the same relationship. In an apt shift from the five beat lines of the first section of the song, which is entirely descriptive of landscape, Callicles uses a tripping storytelling four beat line in the second section to describe the student-teacher, son-father relationship between Achilles and the Centaur who "taught him to explore / The mountains":

> He show'd him Phthia far away,
> And said: O boy, I taught this lore
> To Peleus, in long distant years!
> He told him of the Gods, the stars,
> The tides;—and then of mortal wars,
> And of the life which heroes lead
> Before they reach the Elysian place
> And rest in the immortal mead;
> And all the wisdom of his race.
>   (act 1, sc. 2, 68-76)

Callicles thus sings of the perfect relationship between the old and the new, the father and the son, the master of all song and his student, in words strikingly similar to those he uses to conclude the poem with an emphasis upon the poet who combines in his art both the mythical and the historical, the heavenly and the earthly, the universal and the particular. Arnold's strategy of contrast is clear, for this song is followed immediately by Empedocles' lengthy speech whose primary emphasis is upon the rejection of myth, of illusion, of story, against a background of reduced expectations of happiness in which he concludes with advice to Pausanias, "Because thou must not dream, thou need'st not then despair," which he himself cannot accept. As dramatic poetry it works beautifully, and the technique of contrast and absorption is carried to the next logical step in Callicles' second song which is preceded by "a long pause" after Empedocles has had his lengthy say.

Now Callicles sings of a myth of transformation in which some ideal merging of two separate personalities and forces occurs in a landscape far away and totally different from the landscape of Etna. In his depiction of the transformation of Cadmus and Harmonia into "two bright and aged snakes" who had seen "the billow of calamity / Over their own dear children roll'd," to whom long ago "the Gods had to their marriage come, / And at the banquet all the Muses sang," and who

> did not end their days
> In sight of blood; but were rapt, far away,
> To where the west-wind plays,
> And murmurs of the Adriatic come
> To those untrodden mountain-lawns; and there
> Placed safely in changed forms, the pair
> Wholly forgot their first sad life, and home,
> And all that Theban woe, and stray
> For ever through the glens, placid and dumb,
>   (act 1, sc. 2, 452-460)

Arnold has Callicles present a counterpattern to Empedocles' movement toward suicide in which the nature of poetry and the nature of myth are revealed to contain the antidote to Empedocles' depression and loss of faith. He suggests in the mythic partnership a relevance to the relationship between the poet and the philosopher. He emphasizes that when all is done the myth comes both first and last; the poetry contains, diminishes, even overwhelms the dry philosophy. Callicles retains poetic language and the ability to structure that language, capacities that Empedocles has lost, as he has lost the capacity for joy. His only response to Callicles' songs is: "That was my harp-player again—where is he? / Down by the stream?" He dismisses Pausanias and turns toward the volcano.

No sooner, at the beginning of act 2, does Empedocles melodramatically insist that he "has come too late" and resolve to "turn thee to the elements, thy friends" than Callicles presents a song appropriate to the mood and occasion. As Empedocles poises to plunge into the crater, Callicles sings a variant of the myth of Typho, whose rebellion against Zeus produced a punishment that engendered universal groans and permanent bitterness. The voice of Typho is the voice of the volcano, both of which are associated with Empedocles whose groans and complaints have immediately preceded Callicles' song. The major emphasis is upon the "lyre's voice" which "is lovely everywhere" but "only to Typho it sounds hatefully." Gloomy, discordant Typho is contrasted with a Dryden-like universal harmony which is meant to emphasize the disparity between the depressed disharmonious Empedocles and the joyful harmonious Callicles, the failed historical Romantic poet and the mythic ideal Romantic poet. The contrast is one not meant to disparage Empedocles; it is a depiction of things as they are, or at least as Arnold saw them, indeed as many of his Romantic predecessors saw them. In emphasizing the gap between the different conditions of the model and the actuality, Arnold is attempting to show modern man, or Romantic man, against the background of the anxieties of modern society:

> Hast thou sworn, in thy sad lair,
> Where erst the strong sea-currents suck'd thee down,
> Never to cease to writhe, and try to rest,
> Letting the sea-stream wander through thy hair?
> That thy groans, like thunder prest,
> Begin to roll, and almost drown
> The sweet notes whose lulling spell
> Gods and the race of mortals love so well,
> When through thy caves thou hearest music swell?
>
> (act 2, 58-66)

Arnold in much the same imagery has presented similar situations in other poems, and Coleridge's warning to "Beware! Beware! / His flashing eyes, his floating hair" is one that Arnold took seriously.

A rather short speech by Empedocles, in which he grants that Callicles "fables, yet speaks truth" and in which he renounces magic, his "golden circlet, / My purple robe," immediately follows the conclusion of the third song, in which Callicles has emphasized that in Olympus the groans of Typho can hardly be heard above the universal harmony. As if in response to this renunciation of the magic of art, in his fourth song Callicles sings of the divided self, of the three singers, in the myth of the competition between Marsyas and Apollo which the young Olympus observes. Though Pausanias is the literal physician of the poem, it is Callicles who is the best diagnostician of Empedocles' illness and who can use poetry that tells a story, that combines lyric intensity with "action," to depict in a non-personal, non-subjective way the condition of Empedocles' soul.

Marsyas, in conspiracy with Pan, aspires to defeat Apollo in a competition for poetic supremacy. The Muses are to be the judges. The Maenads and the young Olympus, Marsyas' friend, are to be the observers. In the competition on the lyre, the implacable, youthful, haughty Apollo defeats Marsyas, the Faun, whom "Apollo's minister / Hanged upon a branching fir . . . / and began to whet his knife." The Maenads attempt to intervene on the Faun's behalf, Apollo rebuffs them, and

> *Therefore now Olympus stands,*
> *At his master's piteous cries*
> *Pressing fast with both his hands*
> *His white garment to his eyes,*
> *Not to see Apollo's scorn;—*
> *Ah, poor Faun, poor Faun! ah, poor Faun!*
> (act 2, 185-190)

The artist figure is divided into three: the non-human god of art, his more fallible challenger, and the pupil of the challenger. Marsyas is roughly similar to Empedocles, the failed artist, while Olympus compares to Callicles in his role as student who must stand aside and watch the pain and suffering of his master. Apollo represents the somewhat inhuman, unforgiving, and amorally ruthless force of creativity that connects man to divinity, that in its awesomeness and mystery seems simultaneously both creative and destructive. He is Arnold's version of Blake's "fearful symmetry," of the confident, merciless creator of the tiger and of the tiger itself. The supreme model of confident creativity, like Keats's nightingale, Apollo's presence can only serve to emphasize the gap between the fallible and defeated artist and his image of creative fulfillment, between Empedocles and Callicles, between the aspirations of many Romantic and Victorian poets and their own doubting and pessimistic assessment of their achievements. As much as any major nineteenth-century poet, Arnold felt the loss of creative confidence, the anxieties of the diminished sense of self as poet, and expressed the loss in his poems. The lament for the "poor Faun" is partially a lament for the suffering Empedocles. It is also a disguised and objectified lament for the suffering poet, Arnold himself.

As he has done before, Callicles creates myths or stories that are more true and pertinent to the condition of Empedocles than any direct facts could be. Empedocles seems to recognize the relevance of the story, for in the first words he speaks after the song's conclusion he not only continues his statement of renunciation of magic but intensifies it, revealing that he is aware of the significance of the "poor Faun." In his most explicit statement in the drama, he renounces his "laurel bough, / Scornful Apollo's ensign," expresses his rejection of the Romantic ethos, both its imagery and its values, emphasizes that he is "dead to life and joy," and moves towards the possible revitalization of his spirit in the energetic, boiling, "sea of fire." His "plunge into the volcano" is followed by Callicles' fifth song which makes the final comment of the poem, illustrating again in the dramatic structure of the poem that Empedocles is a temporal phase enclosed within the eternal Callicles.

Arnold's use of the dramatic mode and of devices of contrast in the poem's structure reveals his divided mind and seems a conscious attempt not to reconcile or solve in an extra-poetic way the problems with which he deals in "Empedocles on Etna." [20] He seems to flee from the Romantic poet's subjective commitment to the visionary truth and his assertion of the value of his art, to a kind of tense dramatic fence-sitting in which the surface objectivity of the dramatic form is intended to keep the issue hanging. Arnold strongly leaned in the direction of Callicles, and the poem's structure reinforces this predilection, though, perhaps, given the quality of this work as a comment on the complex mystery of creativity and the creator, it ought not to be put in these competitive terms at all. Indeed, Empedocles and Callicles are different phases in the world history of the same phenomenon. That we begin and end with Callicles is a result of the larger view of this phenomenon, which somehow Arnold was able to glimpse even amidst his crisis of vocation. In Callicles' final song, we are given an example of the possible transformation, like the transformation of Cadmus and Harmonia into "two bright and aged snakes," of "the mind turned in upon itself" into the positive and creative "act of the mind." Callicles sings:

> *First hymn they the Father*
> *Of all things; and then,*
> *The rest of the immortals,*
> *The action of men.*
>
> *The day in his hotness,*
> *The strife with the palm;*
> *The night in her silence,*
> *The stars in their calm.*
> (act 2, 461-468)

Wallace Stevens concludes "Of Modern Poetry" with a parallel comment on what shall be the subject for poetry in our time, though, significantly, the transcendent element has disappeared completely.[21] Only the emphasis on things as they are remains:

> *The actor is*
> *A metaphysician in the dark, twanging*
> *An instrument, twanging a wiry string that gives*
> *Sounds passing through sudden rightness, wholly*
> *Containing the mind, below which it cannot descend,*
> *Beyond which it has no will to rise.*
> *It must*
> *Be the finding of a satisfaction, and may*

> Be a man skating, a woman dancing, a woman
> Combing. The poem of the act of the mind.

The integrity of "Empedocles on Etna" affirms the value of Arnold's conflicts and anxieties. Yet, the enigma of Arnold, like that of Coleridge, still remains. Can anyone ever demonstrate that it was desirable to solve these anxieties instead of dramatizing them over and over again in "a series of Empedoclean victories?" Did not Arnold the man have the right as partial shaper of his own destiny to do so? Can it indeed be shown that poetic sterility necessarily followed from his obsession with culture and progress? For those for whom "poetry" counts above everything else, Arnold went wrong somewhere. For those who believe that contribution to society transcends the satisfactions of art, Arnold, whether voluntarily or not, made the right decision. For those who have not and may never make up their minds, or who hope for some reconciliation between the extremes, the human drama embodied in the poem adds to the mystery of Arnold's art.

10

Parallel Kings and Singers

FOR BROWNING, ARNOLD was always "dear Mat Arnold," and Arnold's image of "two bright and aged snakes" in Callicles' second song was a personal favorite that Browning used often in his correspondence to describe the fanciful retirement-transformation of himself and Isa Blagden.[1] In his note to "Empedocles" in the 1867 edition of his poems, Arnold offered Browning's admiration for the poem as justification for its republication, as if the critical-moral scruples he had expressed to explain its omission from the 1853 volume no longer mattered. Indeed, Browning has seldom been more charming than when he wrote that "I should like to know something about Arnold's new volume: he told me he had reprinted therein 'Empedocles on Etna'—with a pretty note saying it

was done thro' my request. I am really flattered at *that*—I like the
man as much as his poems." [2]

But when Browning persuaded Arnold to republish "Empedocles on Etna," he also tacitly acknowledged that his admiration
was based both on a profound sympathy for the dramatic form and
a deep identification with the central situation of the poem. A recent critic suggests that the influence may have gone both ways,
that "the spectacle of what happened to Empedocles in 1852 led
[Browning] to rescue Saul in 1855," just as "it is barely possible that
Arnold was influenced by the first part of this poem, which was
published in 1845." [3] Whether or not Browning read "Empedocles" in the October 1852 edition in time to be influenced in the
completion of "Saul" in the winter of 1852-53 has not yet been determined, though it seems very likely.[4] Yet the striking parallels between the two poems and their ultimately contrasting visions say a
great deal about both poets' incorporation of their concern with
poetry, the poet, and the creative process into the structure and imagery of their poems.

As Callicles is Arnold's version of the Romantic lyric poet attempting to use music as medicine to cure his philosopher-king, so
too David is Browning's version of a similar singer with a similar
mission. Both Saul and Empedocles suffer from a "sickness unto
death," the ultimate Romantic malaise which results from some
loss of creativity and commitment which can never be defined precisely, but often in Romantic poetry is connected directly to the
poet's loss of ability to *feel* creative, often to feel at all. Then the
world takes on the coloration of the internal mood of the poet or
his character, black, gloomy, and without "joy." Such is the case
with Empedocles, for the world, Arnold tells us, is not out of joint;
the dislocation of the universe has been imposed upon phenomena
that could provide evidence of stability when seen through less despairing eyes.

Many Romantic and Victorian poems begin with a mood of
extreme depression because the artist has lost faith in his own creative power and in the creative power in the universe at large. But
Browning's interest in projective psychology and fictional creation,
as well as his preoccupation with a kind of Christian existentialism,

moves him in his depiction of Saul considerably further away than Arnold from this traditional Romantic emphasis on the artist's loss of personal creativity and his general loss of confidence in universal harmony. Saul, indeed, unlike Empedocles, is not a poet or musician, though he is of the same kingly cast, and Browning's initial and major emphasis is on his spiritual-theological crisis in which ultimately the origin of his "sickness unto death" is his loss of faith, not in himself but in God's love for man and His gift of personal immortality. The ultimate success of David in curing Saul, in contrast to Callicles' failure with Empedocles, derives from the fact that Saul's problem is a spiritual-theological one; it can be ministered to by discursive argument, by spiritual and theological "logic";[5] Empedocles' illness comes from himself and reverts to himself, having no touchstones or relevancy to external laws, institutions, or generally held beliefs. The possible insufficiencies of external reality infect Saul alone; the internal insufficiencies of Empedocles infect the universe at large. Browning has faith in a vague kind of nondenominational Christianity in which characters can mold, can create, their own identity and live morally heroic lives in the acceptance of the analogical if not the literal truth of the central Christian doctrines of the Incarnation, the Resurrection, and the existence of a God of Love whose love for man is so great that He could not deny him immortality. Between 1845 and 1855, this belief seems to have crystallized in Browning; in 1852-53, and even in 1867, Arnold had no such theological commitment.

To a striking degree, "Saul," like Browning's poems on art and artists taken as a group and like "Empedocles," is also about the relationship between the successful and the unsuccessful poet. Saul's illness is a variation of the traditional Romantic melancholy and depression with which so many major Romantic poems begin.[6] David's "ministry" is to discover and make articulate the power of creativity and joy in the universe at large, which will awaken within the king his own lost capacity for finding meaning and significance in "things as they are," in the joys of this world. As for Empedocles, so too for Saul, the pleasures of this world cannot offer incentives for the continuation of action and life against a background of universal disharmony in which, for Empedocles, the social environment has rejected his values and in which, for Saul, the other-worldly basis for this world's pleasures has disappeared. Callicles' glorification of nature in act 1, scene 1, of "Empedocles" has its parallel in David's glorification of nature and emphasis upon its underlying universal moral harmony in sections V-IX of "Saul." The parallel carries forward from substance to results: for both singers are initially unsuccessful in restoring their patients through song. As both Callicles and Empedocles represent polarized aspects of Arnold within an internal drama, so also do David and Saul represent polarized aspects of the artist as Browning sees him: on the one hand, the artist of Romantic despair and melancholy, who has lost all power to create, to sing; on the other, the youthful and subjective Shelley-like Romantic lyricist whose song captures the essence of the ultimate substance of the universe, reconciling, indeed harmonizing, the earthly and the heavenly, man and god.[7]

This is not an uncommon theme in Browning's poetry, especially between 1840 and 1855, except that normally Browning did not combine both poet archetypes into a single poem, preferring to deal with them individually, a pattern quite consistent with the needs of the dramatic monolog form. His earliest dramatic poems, particularly *Paracelsus*, present characters who represent these contrasting types. As Browning's involvement with the dramatic monolog became more intense, as his commitment to acting out, at least on the surface, the role of "objective" poet became more firm, his general tendency was to concentrate upon the failed artist, the melancholy or the numbed or the totally discredited creator, in single poems devoted entirely to the point of view of the major character. Callicles, David, Ariel, Shelley, the lyric Browning, all take a secondary place to the unknown painter of "Pictor Ignotus," to Andrea del Sarto, to the poet of "Dis Aliter Visum," and to all the other artist and quasi-artist failures of Browning's poetry, among whom Fra Lippo Lippi is a notable exception. When Browning writes a dramatic narrative, as he does in "Saul,"[8] he is able to deal with the tension between contrasts in a way that he could not in dramatic monologs, just as Arnold was more successful in depicting the tensions within himself in the dramatic than in the lyric form.

In a general way, there is a parallel between the fruitless attempts of the Romantics to write epic and the attempts of the Victorians to write formal drama rather than dramatic monologs or lyric poetry. Arnold ceased to attempt "modern" drama when he ceased to be a poet. Browning, after an early period of concentrated effort to write drama, made the attempt in a periphrastic way a number of times in his mature career. Tennyson, of course, attempted and failed dismally all his life to find formal dramatic expression for personal and historical themes. Browning's appreciation, then, for "Empedocles on Etna" may have had as much to do with his and his contemporaries' interest in the developed drama as a form, as with his own struggles with a relationship very much like that between Callicles and Empedocles.

Because Browning wrote the first nine sections of "Saul" in 1845 and the remaining ten sections "probably . . . during the winter of 1852-53," it generally has been assumed that he was able to complete the poem because of the development of his religious views during this momentous period in his life.[9] But this hardly explains the unity of the poem and the connection between the earlier and later sections. Most of Browning's "Saul" presents directly the words of David, the narrator, who tells a story in which his own address to Saul predominates. It is basically a therapeutic exhortation, an attempt to use language to cure the sick king, just as the poem is mainly, like Wordsworth's "Tintern Abbey," a therapeutic poem. Browning intends his poem to be to its readers what David's song is to Saul: an exorcism, a stimulant, and a vehicle of personal resurrection and rebirth. The earlier sections of the poem use concrete images of this earth, of things as they are, to justify and catalyze human existence; the later sections use abstract images of things as they should be, of "law" and "love," to explain and give meaning to human life. The contrast between nature and the supernatural, between man and God, is one that Browning, unlike Arnold, could reconcile, even in the structure of his poem.

In the first section, David, who is not placed in local time and space until section XIV, quotes Abner on the seriousness of Saul's condition, the king's illness creating deprivation and withdrawal from life for all his subjects:

> *Neither drunken nor eaten have we; nor until from*
> *his tent*
> *Thou return with the joyful assurance the King*
> *liveth yet,*
> *Shall our lip with the honey be bright, with the*
> *water be wet. . . .*

(section I)

His sickness is an internal one, best represented by the image of the soul or the imagination struggling with itself. Some powerful demonic force, like the Romantic storm in which the negative side of creativity predominates, has overwhelmed Saul, just as a deep depression and melancholy have overcome innumerable Romantic voices, just as "a great melancholy . . . with dreams and darkness" has taken possession of Merlin in "Merlin and Vivien." Outside, Abner tells David, a "wild heat" is "now raging to torture the desert." For Saul, and for those within the contagious area of his infection, life is an internal and external wasteland of despair and threatening destruction.

Saul, David tells us in section III, is like Christ on the cross at the moment of loss of conviction in his divine component: in a kind of "darkness visible." He is "more black than the blackness," David says, seeing Saul spread-eagled in crucifixion position against the "main prop which sustains the pavilion." In a touch that suggests an indebtedness to his museum-visiting in Italy and England prior to his long residence in Italy after 1845, Browning shows us, through David's eyes, the Renaissance-Biblical sunbeam which "burst thro' the tent-roof, showed Saul." Yet, at the same time as Saul is Christ, he is also God the father, the philosopher-king, the authority figure, the giant of a creator and artist reduced not, as Blake would have it, in size, but in power. David is "thy servant," an embodiment of divine love, universalizing and democratizing the hierarchy between "suffering servants" so that God and Christ, God and Man, are one and the same through the power of love. Yet, in section IV, the Christ-imagery is intensified and transformed:

> *He stood as erect as that tent-prop, both arms*
>   *stretched out wide*
> *On the great cross-support in the centre, that*
>   *goes to each side. . . .*

Browning exploits, as he does in "Childe Roland to the Dark Tower Came," the primitive-mythological substructure of Christianity to universalize further his psychological situations:

> *He relaxed not a muscle, but hung there as,*
>   *caught in his pangs*
> *And waiting his change, the king-serpent all*
>   *heavily hangs,*
> *Far away from his kind, in the pine, till*
>   *deliverance come*
> *With the spring-time,—so agonized Saul, drear*
>   *and stark, blind and dumb.*
>   (section IV)

A recent critic has emphasized that Biblical "type" plays an important role in "Saul." [10] But Saul is more than a character whose typology is Biblical. He is the blind Samson and the crucified Christ. He is also the slain summer King, the wounded Fisher-King, and a representative of all those pre-Christian types dramatized by literary anthropologists since *The Golden Bough* and best symbolized by the oddly modern and Lawrentian image of "the king-serpent" waiting to shed his old skin and be reborn.

David's song, then, first begins in section V, and in its emphasis on the manifestation of the spiritual in the material, of God or the life-force of the universe in nature, has much in common with the general burden of "Tintern Abbey" and the opening speeches of Callicles in act 1, scene 1, of "Empedocles on Etna." Like Callicles, he sings, "What mortal could be sick or sorry here?" Also, like Callicles, he discovers that the obvious answer to this rhetorical question is contradicted by reality. Both Empedocles and Saul have illnesses that are not amenable to the therapy of nature. Yet Saul is ultimately cured because the vision of nature presented by David

is, for Browning, an accurate one, though the initial presentation
has only minor effect on Saul. It is not God in nature that is in
question for Saul but a God of love in the universe, and his illness
has progressed so radically that indirect contact with God through
nature will not effect the cure. Only direct contact of a visionary
sort will suffice. Callicles, however, has no such therapeutic success,
for, within the context of Arnold's poem, it is quite clear that there
is no conviction on the author's part that what Callicles says is true,
that nature restores. Of course, Arnold's convictions and his classical framework allow him to have Callicles omit completely the pan-
theistic element in nature on which Browning relies. Nature is
beautiful, friendly, ennobling, and therapeutic, Callicles says, but
there is no indication that it is moral and that it manifests and is
controlled by a beneficent divine force. The "pass in the forest re-
gion of Etna" is a natural paradise and all that can be concluded
from Callicles' naturalistic description is that no one *should* be sick
in these surroundings but that someone *is*. David, however, who
moves from songs of domesticated flocks in section V to songs of
the small wild creatures of the fields in section VI, concludes:

> *God made all the creatures and gave them our love*
> > *and our fear,*
> *To give sign, we and they are his children, one*
> > *family here.*

David, incorrectly gauging the depth and the direction of Saul's illness, wants to "buttress an arch / Nought can break" by demon-
strating that in the progression of life up the ladder or around the
chain of being God is manifest in all elements. Having done with
the creatures, he now turns to man.

David sings of the substantial and cyclical pleasures of this
world, emphasizing the significance and the satisfactions of work,
friendship, and a noble and praised completion of life. Death is the
natural completion of life, he tells Saul, calling attention to its cyclical processes, emphasizing both its continuity and the continuity
of its institutions. The song of loss and separation is followed by a
hymn to marriage and climaxed by David's typically Victorian em-

phasis on "the great march / Wherein man runs to man to assist him and buttress an arch / Nought can break." We find life's meaning in action, in social commitment, in being a member of the community of man, "and grow one in the sense of this world's life."

That part of Saul's illness manifests itself in a loss of feeling becomes clear in section VIII, suggesting a further parallel with all those Romantics who cannot feel. Keats's "drowsy numbness" and Coleridge's "dull pain . . . a grief without a pang, void, dark, and drear" is echoed in "so agonized Saul, drear and stark, blind and dumb" (section IV). Saul is experiencing death-in-life, both the loss of faith or mission that haunts the ancient mariner through his voyage and the traditional paradox that permits the Romantic to suffer intensely while at the same time his death-in-life and his suffering are caused by loss of feeling. David "paused, held [his] breath in such silence, and listened apart; / And the tent shook, for mighty Saul shuddered. . . ." A success so minimal it is only amenable to the measurement of a shudder has been achieved, and David is encouraged to resume his song. In section IX, he continues at length the emphasis of section VII. Browning has never been a more convincing advocate of the joys of this life. David sings of "the wild joys of living": physical vigor, food, sleep, health, exercise, battle, trust, friendship, growth, maturity, accomplishment, and fame. And the result is positive:

> *One long shudder thrilled*
> *All the tent till the very air tingled, then sank*
> *and was stilled*
> *At the King's self left standing before me,*
> *released and aware.*
> *What was gone, what remained? All to traverse,*
> *'twixt hope and despair;*
> *Death was past, life not come. . . .*
>
> (section X)

That is the extent of the therapeutic power of the first part of David's song, of his emphasis upon the satisfactions of this life as justification for living and as catalyst for joy. For Saul's illness is such that he cannot make the assertive leap from the realities of earth to the assumptions of heaven. The process must work the other way. Ultimately, Browning's message is that the inspired poet under the proper conditions can embody the pure visionary insight in song and communicate the essence of the "white light." David joins heaven and earth as Browning unites the two divisions of his poem. Whereas, in the first, David ministers to the soul through a vision of earth, in the second, he does so through a vision of heaven. Though it is not Saul's body that is sick, the connection between body and soul permits David's first song to turn Saul's body away from death but not to turn his soul toward life. Saul resumes his "habitudes kingly" and forsakes his crucifixion position as David sings, first, of the immortality that comes from great deeds and is embodied in the written memory of the race, then, of the Christian dispensation that is to come. David transcends song in a process in which song disappears, very different from the ascension of song towards pure lyric utterance typified, for example, by Keats's nightingale and Shelley's skylark:

> Then the truth came upon me. No harp more—
> no song more! outbroke
>
> (section XVI)

In sections XVII-XIX, the seer, David, through some special dispensation, cures Saul of his "sickness unto death" by revealing in utterance the future but always existent testimony that, through Christ, God loves man so intensely that He could never deny him the possibility of that immortality in which he, Browning feels, so desperately needs to believe. The poem concludes with David's description of the entire natural world testifying to the universal validity and power of his vision; "the new law" has been revealed even to "the startled wild beasts" who seem to recognize that God is more powerful than Darwin. Obviously, Browning has departed rather significantly from the context of "Empedocles on Etna" as, it is safe to assume, he had every intention of doing.[11]

Still, the words of sections VII and IX of "Saul" echo the con-

clusion of Empedocles' sermon on the mount to Pausanias, though
Empedocles' actions indicate that he does not have the same deep
commitment as David to this vision of the sufficiency of earthly
things; and, of course, for Empedocles, nature does not provide evidence to indicate that "God made all the creatures":

> *Is it so small a thing*
> *To have enjoy'd the sun,*
> *To have lived light in the spring,*
> *To have loved, to have thought, to have done;*
> *To have advanced true friends, and beat down*
> >   *baffling foes.*

(act 1, sc. 2, ll. 397-401)

It is not "so small a thing," but then neither is it a very great thing
for Empedocles. Ultimately David's celebration of the joys of this
earth, predicated on the inextricable connection between earth and
heaven, man and God, finds a more thorough parallel in Callicles'
final song. He connects the lower and the higher, the story of man
and the story of God, in Arnold's strangely brilliant and non-Chris-
tian version of what Browning did when he conceived "Saul" as a
two-part unified ascension from man's world to God's world.

Both David and Callicles are subjective poets of pure vision,
who see the cyclical movement and connection between all
things.[12] Callicles concludes at a point which parallels what David
sings in section VII, includes more briefly what David incorporates
into section IX, emphasizes the importance of the relationship between the human and the divine as a subject for poetry which is implicit in David's entire address to Saul, but completely omits any
anticipations of Christian theology. For David, the object of song
is vision and redemption; for Callicles, the object of song is pleasure in singing:

> *'Tis Apollo comes leading*
> *His choir, the Nine.*
> *—The leader is fairest,*
> *But all are divine.*

.   .   .   .   .   .

First hymn they the Father
Of all things; and then,
The rest of immortals,
The action of men.

The day in his hotness,
The strife with the palm;
The night in her silence,
The stars in their calm.
(act 2, ll. 445-468)

Implicit in Callicles' association of himself with Apollo and his choir is his assumption of his own immortality through song. The Romantic poet has always dared suggest not only that through his art he could see the divine but that he himself as maker identified with and perhaps even became God.[13] Blake's poetry best represents this position, but there are elements of it, both as aspiration and as threat, in Wordsworth, Keats, Shelley, and Coleridge especially. Immortality and divinity for Browning are things very distinct from poetry, and David's divinity comes not from his function as poet but from his function as poetic vehicle of the Christian revelation. Though these poets flourish as arms of the same tree, the branches are different. If Callicles has the final triumph in "Empedocles," and David in "Saul," the former is a triumph for poetry, the latter for religion through poetry. Both represent variations of and a decline in the Romantic commitment to poetry as the subject of poems and the poet as the hero of his own poems, a commitment which, despite varying fortunes, has flourished remarkably and perhaps enduringly in the twentieth century. Paradoxically, and this is the irony of much Romantic poetry, both are great achievements in the Romantic tradition. But the self depicted here has become a more confused and less insistently self-affirming force, abandoning the comparatively direct confrontation and exploration of lyric for the minor safeguards of monolog, drama, and religious vision. Indeed, Arnold and Browning, despite the brilliance of their poetic strategies, can hardly avoid revealing that two of the major subjects of their poetry are their anxieties about their sense of themselves as poets and their uneasiness about the role of poetry in creating, defining, and revealing itself and them.

11

Conclusion

THESE CHAPTERS HAVE offered an interpretation of the Romantic ethos in nineteenth-century English poetry, emphasizing the dominance of self-concern among its poets, both Romantic and Victorian. After this time, the complexity of psychological, biographical, and aesthetic correlatives that were subsumed into the major poems of the period could never be disentangled completely again. For such is the very nature of poetry that it has only the illusive clarity of a very fragile and complex form of human expression. But since poetry is of such a nature and is of such paramount importance for our lives and for the life of our culture, we must each examine for ourselves the tradition of which our major poetry is part, that it in fact has created. For, in a special sense, just as the Romantics and Victorians created a series of myths and symbols out of which their poems came, created a literary tradition and consequently a heritage which focused on the poet's concern for his own creativity and the nature of poetry within his poems, so too we create a tradition in our arrangements and interpretations of the poetry of the past. What I have tried to do in this study is to arrange and interpret some portion of the legacy bequeathed to us by nineteenth-century poetry and to order and structure a myth that may become part of the tradition we pass on.

In brief, the Romantic and Victorian poets focus in some of their major poems on the poet's own image of himself and his art. Though the tendency can hardly be graphed with any unswervable certainties of decline, generally as the century advances there is a sometimes gradual, sometimes abrupt, plunge in self-confidence about the poet, his mission, and the function of poetry in society. Blake begins the Romantic tradition with a sweeping affirmation of the powers of the poet, inseparable from his own image of himself as a creator with deific powers, and expresses with sublime self-confidence the harmony of the visionary poet with the true facts of the universe. Of all the Romantics and Victorians, only Blake refuses to distinguish between vision and creation, so committed is he to the inextricable relationship between visionary experience and artistic expression. For the visionary Blake, the only Romantic the radical consciousness of the nineteen-seventies finds radical enough, seems in "The Tyger" to be celebrating the poet and his powers as much as the experience of dreadful but liberating apocalypse. For Blake, vision and creation are the same; so any vision is a vision of making, of the poet or visionary forging the poem in the smithy of his soul. And Blake's particular way of making poems is through vision, imaginative insight framed in metaphors and communicated in words to express part or all of the total scheme of things as he sees it. That he is less self-conscious than the poets who follow him in the Romantic and Victorian tradition of concern within poetry for the problems of poet and poem is a distinction that hardly removes him from connection with the "splendour in the grass" and "the weariness, the fever, and the fret" that follow in the anxieties of poets more acutely aware of their own self-concern.

It could be said that Blake's concern for poetry was so much a part of his concern for all things, was indeed so inextricably connected to a larger synthesis, that rarely does he isolate it as a subject, either in his letters, his prose, or his poetry.

Lyric forms tend to be his major means of expressing such certitudes, and they are also, for the Romantics, major ways of expressing incertitude and even doubt and despair. The form that the Romantics invent, the greater Romantic lyric or the Romantic meditative ode, directly expresses in its flexibility, circularity, and emotional directness the willingness of the Romantic poet to speak in his own voice of both his ecstasy and his pain. Wordsworth in "Tintern Abbey" and Coleridge in "Frost at Midnight" express their attitudes towards creativity and themselves as poets as well as towards the very nature of poetry, at the particular points in their emotional and aesthetic careers that these poems represent. For Wordsworth, the affirmation of "Tintern Abbey" is matched by that of a long series of poems that cover most of his poetic career, with "Ode: Intimations of Immortality on Recollections from Early Childhood" and The Prelude high points in that tradition. For Coleridge, "Frost at Midnight" is a comparatively rare affirmation of poetic possibilities, containing within itself the seeds of doubt and renunciation that grew with luxuriant perverseness in "Dejection: An Ode" and turned him eventually to forms of self-expression other than poetry.

In form, the movement between 1790 and 1864 is from subjective lyric toward objective narrative and dramatic monolog. The greater Romantic lyric is normally a poem of direct authorial involvement in which a consciousness which we associate with the poet focuses on some specific situation in which time past and time present, this special place, and these particular feelings and thoughts are brought together to cohere as co-functions, often as interchangeable representatives of the poet's view of himself and his world. Though Blake as satirist has many masks, in "The Tyger" he clearly speaks directly as prophetic poet, without the mediation of a special voice or a special dramatic stance, and both Wordsworth in "Tintern Abbey" and Coleridge in "Frost at Midnight" and "Dejection: An Ode" make every effort to confront and reveal themselves directly. The voice of the poem is the voice of the poet, and the fully developed Romantic meditative ode as practiced by Wordsworth, Coleridge, Keats, and Shelley, despite the suicidal depression that may be at the heart of the poet's mood, makes every effort to avoid indirectness and evasiveness in point of view, indeed emphasizes the direct responsibility of the poet for the utterance.

Wordsworth intends "Tintern Abbey" to be a "kindred mutation," to provide for the reader the same kind of release and revitalization that nature provides for the poet. And the major subject of the poem is the relationship between nature, the poet, the poem, and the reader. In a sense, then, the poem is about creativity and the creative process in which "these my exhortations" are the permanent forms of potential revitalization that the poet has created for his sister Dorothy and for all those who read his words in the future. Except for Shelley, only Blake and Wordsworth among nineteenth-century poets manage this degree of self-confidence about their powers as poets and the specific positive mission of their poetry. Shelley in "Ode to the West Wind" and particularly in "To a Skylark," though a degree of anxiety underlies the occasionally frenetic and nervous implorations that contrasts with Wordsworth's comparatively calm and charismatic exhortations, shares some of the Wordsworthian self-confidence and is able to work out in these poems an imagistic and structural formula that seems to suggest fulfillment and self-assertion. Wordsworth clearly intends "Tintern Abbey" to be not only a record of his own rebirth but also a cure for those, like Coleridge and Keats, who have lost "the passion and the life whose fountains are within." Wordsworth would have been pleased to have learned of the therapeutic role his poetry played in restoring John Stuart Mill to a commitment to life, of turning the "melancholy winter" into a new spring.

For Coleridge, however, anxiety concerning his powers as a poet and the efficacy of his poetry dominated his major years of creativity and many of his poems, including "Frost at Midnight," "Kubla Khan," "The Ancient Mariner," and "Dejection: An Ode." But "Frost at Midnight" is a rare achievement, the only poem of Coleridge's in which the demons of self-doubt are momentarily conquered and properly subordinated to the overall requirements of a poem whose major theme is the reawakening of the sleeping poet, the revitalization of creativity, the reconciliation of opposites within poetry, and the hope of creativity in future generations. Much of Coleridge's career anticipates Keats's and Arnold's. For Coleridge, even within the comparative optimism of "Frost at Midnight," blessings are always for someone else. And for Keats, blessings are always to be pursued fruitlessly. The nightingale is always unattainable, and the sense of unfulfilled expectations, of deep self-doubt and anxiety about the functions of the poet and poetry, that run through "Dejection: An Ode" also dominate "Ode to a Nightingale." Like Arnold in "Empedocles on Etna" approximately fifty years later, both poets depict the paralytic instability and loss of feeling that anxiety and self-doubt have produced.

The formal structures of the Romantics, however, proved uncongenial to the Victorians, who, though they shared the same basic concern with creativity and its problems, faced a very different set of internal and external conditions that sent them on a search for more objective and less self-revealing formal structures. They transformed the Romantic meditative ode into the objective narrative and the dramatic monolog. But the concerns remained the same. Perhaps because their generation preferred privacy to publicity, duty to indulgence, prose to poetry, the Victorians sought a poetic form that would not restrict them in their explorations of themselves and what they were as poets but would disguise and even hide the self that is at the center of their poems.

Tennyson's "Locksley Hall" represents an intermediary step in the development of the subjective lyric, in which the poet speaks to us in his own voice, into the objective form in which fictional character and even plot present configurations that substitute for direct utterance. But the basic concern of the poet about his creativity remained the same throughout the century despite the change in the form of presentation, though indeed it can be argued that the Romantic meditative ode is not changed but transformed, like the transformation of Arnold's Cadmus and Harmonia into "two bright and aged snakes" who "played safely in changed forms." Unlike the lovers, the Victorians could not "wholly" forget

> *their first sad life, and home,*
> *And all that Theban woe, and stray*
> *For ever through the glens, placid and dumb.*
> ("Empedocles," act 1, sc. 2, 456-460)

On the contrary, the self-consciousness of the Victorians was extreme, and the mark of its extremity is the effort of craftsmanship they made to conceal it behind the masks of invention. The failure of "Locksley Hall" is the inability of Tennyson to decide just how far he wants to move along the road toward dramatic monolog. The narrator is neither Tennyson nor not Tennyson, a creature who has neither the emotional directness of representing the author nor the objective dignity and individuality of a separate fictional creation. Nevertheless, it is testimony to Tennyson's powers that he is able to do so much with such confusion, almost as if one of the unintended strengths of the poem is its depiction of a character caught between two worlds in a poem caught between two poetic forms or at least caught in the shadows between two phases of a moon that is changing.

Tennyson reveals that he has begun the search in "Locksley Hall" and that the search has been rewarded in "Merlin and Vivien" and in *Idylls of the King*, a poem as much about the poet and his fear of his loss of creativity as about the battle between sense and soul. In "Merlin and Vivien" the depth of Tennyson's self-doubt becomes clear. For in that poem Merlin is depicted as a great artificer, the archetypal artist, who has created a chair in which

> *"No man could sit but he should lose himself."*
> *And once by misadvertence Merlin sat*
> *In his own chair, and so was lost . . . .*
> ("The Holy Grail," ll. 174-176)

But this was far from misadvertence, for Merlin's capitulation to Vivien is a surrender to his own self-doubts, just as Andrea del Sarto's enslavement to Lucrezia is a purposeful renunciation by the artist of his art and a voluntary, suicidal loss of "use and name and fame." Lucrezia, like Vivien to Merlin, is an aspect of Andrea's personality, an internal force to which he has capitulated, in a poem which is one of the most devastating depictions of the failed artist in this Romantic and Victorian tradition.

Objective narrative can use the devices of characterization and plot, of ostensibly fictional setting and even historicism, to relieve the poet of direct identification in his personal life with the public utterances of his creations. Dramatic monolog accomplishes the same end, of course. Some of Browning's most mature and accomplished achievements within that form, "Andrea del Sarto," "Pictor Ignotus," and "Dis Aliter Visum," for example, focus on the same problems of creative anxiety that the Romantics focused on directly fifty or so years earlier. It was one of his favorite themes. The unknown painter of "Pictor Ignotus" is faced with the dilemma that Browning himself confronted after the crushing disappointment of the criticism of his early subjective work. The unknown painter has the capacity to be either subjective lyric poet or objective dramatic poet, like Browning himself. Unlike Browning, however, he chooses neither and turns to the safety of complete withdrawal from artistic competition, as Coleridge and Arnold did when they reconstituted themselves as intellectuals rather than poets. The desiccated and demeaned poet of "Dis Aliter Visum" has also made his choice, the potential Romantic artist has disregarded the demands and implications of his calling and lost not only his art but his soul. This ironic "Byron of our Day," like Andrea, is one of many versions in Browning of the failed artist, suggesting, along with other sources, the deep concern of Browning himself for the problems of creative anxiety and the poet's self-image.

The confident affirmations of the second half of "Saul" reveal one of the directions in which Browning moved to avoid the problems of anxiety and insufficiency, of doubt concerning purpose and mission, that almost inevitably surface in poems that attempt to depict artists. Significantly, Browning seems always to choose to portray failed, not successful, artists and writers. Shelley may have been the "sun-treader," but since Shelley the sun had grown dim.

The religious affirmation of universal harmony in "Saul" is an affirmation of religion through poetry and an attempt to escape the anxieties and frustrations that seem inevitably to accompany all the Victorian attempts to come to grips within poetry with the traditional Romantic theme of the role of the poet and the nature of his art. Perhaps the most comprehensive attempt to deal with the theme is Arnold's "Empedocles on Etna." Though Browning was directly responsible, through his encouragement, for Arnold's republication of the poem, nevertheless the anxieties and failures of the poetic mission directly represented in "Empedocles" are those that Browning eventually tries to escape. Both Callicles and David are Romantic poets who have retained their powers, both Empedocles and Saul fallen singers who have lost their sense of creative mission. But, while David can revive Saul, Callicles can only watch Empedocles plunge into the volcano.

Despite the transformation of the subjective lyric into objective and dramatic forms, the basic imagery of these Romantic and Victorian poems is the same. Naturally. The Victorians closely read their Romantic predecessors, and, though times were indeed changing, they were changing in a way that could only encourage the Victorians to intensify the imagery that naturally belonged to a problem and a theme that both Romantics and Victorians shared. Images in which fire, light, thunder, storm, struggle, wind, and breath are identified with the creative process and the renewal of creativity remain consistently present and functional from Blake to Tennyson. Images in which dullness, darkness, absence of energy, stillness and absence of wind, contained rooms, frames for experience, sensuality, silver and gold represent the atrophy of the creative powers, the loss of commitment to the act of creation, and capitulation to the ways of the world, remain consistently present and dramatically functional throughout nineteenth-century poetry. Empedocles' joylessness is that of Coleridge in "Dejection: An Ode." Andrea del Sarto's loss of feeling is similar to the "drowsy numbness" of Keats's "Ode to a Nightingale." We have similar variants of the creative spirit reviving, sometimes successfully, sometimes not, in Wordsworth's "correspondent breeze," Shelley's "west wind," Tennyson's storms that "rise seaward" in "Locksley Hall" and "Merlin and Vivien," and in Empedocles' ambiguous leap into the volcano.

The symbolic, fertile orderliness of the landscape of "Tintern Abbey" becomes the barren moorland of "Locksley Hall," the threatening and sensual luxuriance of the landscape of "Merlin and Vivien," and the flat, uninteresting lowlands of the dry and desiccated spirit in "Dis Aliter Visum." The great storm of Coleridge's "Dejection: An Ode," which represents the ambiguity of the creative power within the poet and within nature, which threatens destruction yet has within it the hoped for promise of a "mountain-birth," gives birth to the great storms of "Locksley Hall" and "Merlin and Vivien." In the earlier Tennyson poem, the storm is a rather strained expression of rebirth, of new life, of "rain or hail, or fire or snow." The strong blast of the thunderbolt anticipates that "the mighty wind arises, roaring seaward, and I go," an expression of Tennysonian optimism in the possibilities of individual renewal of creativity for the poet and renewal of mission for his country, made explicit later in a similar scene in *Maud.* But, in "Merlin and Vivien," the storm has become totally destructive, an instrument of Vivien's devouring will, of the negative imagination and creativity that she represents as an inseparable part of Merlin's own self. When Merlin becomes imprisoned in the great oak, lost to "use and name and fame," he shares a condition of self-willed imprisonment with the Coleridge of "Frost at Midnight" isolated in his silent room, with Andrea del Sarto locked into the tight, limited, picture-frame prison that he has created for himself, with Empedocles whose mind is turned in upon itself, the ultimate internal prison. One of the most frequent of nineteenth-century images that the Victorians develop from the initiative of the Romantics is the prison-house of the self. Blake, Browning, Coleridge, Wordsworth, Tennyson, Dickens, Bronte, Shaw, Kafka, hardly a major writer since the Romantics, could escape dealing with its enclosures.

Many of these poems attempt to *be* what they are *about,* attempt to present and organize their images and structural elements in such a way as to create in the reader the feeling or emotion the poet is writing about—his fears about his success as an artist, his failures, hopes, and visions as a poet. The Romantic meditative ode is particularly suited to this attempt, for its structure is completely a function of the poet's feelings, totally flexible in line length, stanza length, and poem length, adaptable to the immediate needs of the poet's emotion, perfectly capable of being the subjective vehicle of even extremes of emotion within the same poem. The structure of such a poem is often a graph of the poet's emotional life, and the imagery of such poems often subtly weaves and develops the same pattern, dovetailing perfectly with the structure, as in Coleridge's "Frost at Midnight," in which "the snake with its tail in its mouth" represents both the poem's structural turning in on itself and its imagistic reconciliation of opposites.

But even the objective narratives and monologs of the Victorians reveal the pervasive influence of the Romantics' success in creating poems in which the reader shares in the experience of the poem. As if by some bond of chemical attraction, similar themes creating similar effects, no matter how different the outer form, a good number of Victorian objective poems are thinly disguised presentations by the author of his own concern about his poetic powers and mission. And through effects of repetition, rhythm, imagery, characterization, irony, allegory, even plot, and certainly overall structure, poets like Tennyson, Arnold, and Browning force an emotional experience on their readers the basic characteristic of which is that it is *shared*, that, despite the masks of the objective form, it reveals the author's deep personal concern with his art and that through the devices of poetry it asks, sometimes even pleads, that the reader feel and respond to these same concerns. The greater Romantic lyric or the Romantic meditative ode has undergone a transformation, but its basic themes have been carried forward as an inextricable part of its metamorphosis into objective narrative and monolog.

Of course, the Victorians both suffered from and benefited from their desire to avoid direct association of the reader with the poet and his anxieties, though, for all intents and purposes, since this association is still central to the poems, it often surfaces regardless of how deeply the poet thinks he has buried it. This deep anxiety about the success of the poet as poet often plays just beneath the surface of the purposeful objectivity of many Victorian poems. On rare occasions it comes fully to the fore, and occasionally it is made to seem less threatening by being expressed in prose, as in Browning's essay on Shelley. Even of the Romantics only Wordsworth goes so far, in a discussion of the problem within "Tintern Abbey," as to present a theory of life and poetry based upon the notion that the poem is to be conceived of and constructed in such a way as to play a major role in the life of the reader, to be to the reader very much what nature has been to Wordsworth. In a phrase that he uses in *The Prelude*, poems are to be "kindred mutations," encapsulated and portable reservoirs, like memories, whose cool waters will provide revitalization and rebirth for the reader in a pattern similar to Wordsworth's relationship with nature and memory. And "these my exhortations" that will provide "healing thoughts/ Of tender joy" are the very words of the poem and the processes of emotional responsiveness that will be the reader's to experience whenever he confronts the poem because, indeed, they are built into its structure and images.

Other Romantics, particularly Coleridge and Keats, write poems that are structured to capture, communicate, and recreate in the reader's experience, as he reads, the emotions of anxiety and loss concerning his creativity that the poet deeply feels. But only rarely do these poets find a suitable release from their depression, and it is this alleged stifling of emotional release and catharsis that so concerned Arnold in his rejection of "Empedocles on Etna." So powerfully and effectively has the reader been implicated in the poems in this tradition (and "Empedocles on Etna" reveals the strong influence of "Dejection: An Ode"), and so infrequently has the reader or the poet found release from the anxieties expressed in the poems, that Arnold seemingly would reject a place for himself in the tradition. For Arnold associates himself not with the triumphant affirmations of Blake and the sustained and stoic affirmations of Wordsworth but with the plunge into darkness or death or relativistic confusion that seems inevitably to be the result of the pursuit of the nightingale. Only Blake, Wordsworth, and Browning are able to celebrate triumphantly the victory of their versions of poetry, and Browning's celebration in "Saul" is rare in his career. It is as if Coleridge's "Dejection: An Ode" marks a point after which such victories were unusual or fitful, and, as the century advanced, propped up by nationalism or religion or culture or history or myth or utopianism or sex. Perhaps Empedocles' leap into the volcano is the best symbol of the Romantic poet's failure to sustain his commitment to himself as poet in a physically and psychologically hostile environment in which the main assault came from within, from self-doubt concerning personal creativity and the powers of art. In his next reincarnation, Empedocles purified becomes Arnold the critic.

The further development of objective narrative and monolog into a new form, of the sort we see in Browning's *The Ring and the Book*, and its eventual marriage with narrative fiction has not obscured the fact that the theme of creative anxiety remains constant. It suffuses all the transformations. There is a long tradition, beginning with Cervantes and Fielding, of novelists having the problem of writing novels and being novelists as one of their central themes within their fiction. The concern becomes a very tense and anxious one by the end of the nineteenth century. Much of our major fiction since, from Joyce to Nabokov, has concentrated on the anxieties of art and artists. And a great many of our major twentieth-century poets, Eliot, Pound, Stevens, Auden, Frost, and Williams, to name some of the most prominent, have focused on the theme that Wallace Stevens particularly epitomizes in major poems like "An Ordinary Evening in New Haven" and "The Comedian as the Letter C." The best twentieth-century descriptions of the Romantic and Victorian poet's deep sense of doubt and desire for certainty about his own powers and functions appear not in critical prose but, quite appropriately, in Stevens's poetry, in his description, among others, of the poet of "capable imagination" whose achievement has transformed him into a model of fulfillment:

> The villages slept as the capable man went down,
> Time swished on the village clocks and dreams
> > were alive,
> The enormous gongs gave edges to their sounds,
> As the rider, no chevalere and poorly dressed,

> *Impatient of the bells and midnight forms,*
> *Rode over the picket rocks, rode down the road,*
> *And, capable, created in his mind,*
> *Eventual victor, out of the martyrs' bones,*
> *The ultimate elegance: the imagined land.*
>   ("Mrs. Alfred Uruguay")[1]

The major Romantics and Victorians sometimes found their imaginations "capable," but they often feared and distrusted, and even capitulated to, powers and anxieties within themselves that, in their best achievements, brought both great pain and great poetry.

Notes

Chapter 1

1. See Karl Kroeber, *Romantic Narrative Art* (Madison, 1960). For the best discussion of the epic influence on Romantic poetry, see Brian Wilkie, *The Romantic Poets and Epic Tradition* (Madison, 1965), especially Chapter 1. Harold Bloom, "Keats and the Embarrassments of Poetic Tradition," *From Sensibility to Romance*, ed. F. W. Hilles and H. Bloom (New Haven, 1965), pp. 513-525, and *The Ringers in the Towers: Studies in Romantic Tradition* (New York, 1971) illustrate the importance of the problem; and Thomas A. Vogler, *Preludes to Vision: The Epic Venture in Blake, Keats, Wordsworth, and Hart Crane* (California, 1971) carries it into the twentieth century. Many studies of *The Prelude*, among them Abbie F. Potts, *Wordsworth's Prelude: A Study of Its Literary Form* (Ithaca, 1953), deal with the problems of the personal or subjective epic.

2. Josephine Miles, *Eras and Modes in English Poetry* (Berkeley,

1957), Chapters 6 and 7, argues that the ballad is the most characteristic Romantic structure for poetry.

3. No convenient particularized name has yet been given this new lyric form, though M. H. Abrams, "Structure and Style in the Greater Romantic Lyric," Hilles and Bloom, pp. 527-560, has called it the "greater Romantic lyric" and characterized it as a type of poem which combines the meditative aspect of seventeenth-century verse with the emphasis on topography of the late eighteenth century into a lyric, quasi-ode structure. Robert Langbaum, *The Poetry of Experience* (New York, 1957), has emphasized the dramatic element in the Romantic ode or lyric in order to emphasize the lyric element in the dramatic monolog. The phrase I use often in my discussion is "Romantic meditative ode." The word "ode" is, of course, to be taken very loosely; and I am more interested in the general tradition of the form, so important in the nineteenth century, than in a strict application of the term. Many of the poems that Abrams calls "greater Romantic lyrics" are indeed odes, but others that I am interested in, like "Frost at Midnight," "Tintern Abbey," and "Locksley Hall," obviously are not.

4. Ernest Tuveson, *The Imagination as a Means of Grace* (Berkeley, 1960), pp. 193-194.

5. Wallace Stevens, *The Collected Poems of Wallace Stevens* (New York, 1957), p. 240.

6. See R. A. Foakes, *The Romantic Assertion* (London, 1958), John Heath-Stubbs, *The Darkling Plain* (London, 1950), especially Chapter 1, Masao Miyoshi, *The Divided Self: A Perspective on the Literature of the Victorians* (New York, 1969), and Derek Colville, *Victorian Poetry and the Romantic Religion* (Albany, 1970). For a wide-ranging discussion, see Patricia M. Ball, *The Central Self: A Study in Romantic and Victorian Imagination* (London, 1968).

Chapter 2

1. Hazard Adams, *William Blake, A Reading of the Shorter Poems* (Seattle, 1963), pp. 329-332, contains a descriptive bibliography of articles and sections of books that deal with the poem. A recent casebook, *William Blake: The Tyger*, ed. Winston Weathers (Columbus, 1969), focuses solely on "The Tyger." Important new studies that deal with the poem and its reputation are Alicia Ostriker, *Vision and Verse in William Blake* (Madison, 1965), Deborah Dorfman, *Blake in the Nineteenth Century: His Reputation as a Poet from Gilchrist to Yeats* (New Haven, 1969), Morton Paley, *Energy and Imagination: A Study of Blake's Thought* (New York, 1970), and *Blake's Visionary Forms Dramatic*, ed. D. V. Erdman and John E. Grant (Princeton, 1971).

2. Adams, *Discussions of William Blake*, ed. John E. Grant (Boston, 1961), p. 63, suggests that of the two major concerns of "The Tyger," "the unprolific or distorting and the truly creative process in spiritual life . . . the latter is a process equivalent to the process of creation in art. Creation in art is for Blake the renewal of visionary truth."

3. For my text of the poem and other references to Blake, I have used *The Poetry and Prose of William Blake*, ed. D. Erdman and H. Bloom (New York, 1965).

4. John T. Grant, *Discussions*, p. 79. See Jean H. Hagstrum, *William Blake, Poet and Painter* (Chicago, 1964), pp. 83-87.

5. See John B. Beer, *Blake's Humanism* (New York, 1968).

6. See Adams, *Discussions*, p. 56.

7. Fred C. Robinson in "Verb Tense in Blake's 'The Tyger'," *PMLA*, LXXIX (1964), 666-669, argues that the "dare" in the first and final stanzas is a form that could have been used as either past or present tense in the eighteenth century, and that Blake used it as a past tense form. The evidence seems inconclusive.

8. See M. H. Abrams, "The Correspondent Breeze: A Romantic Metaphor," *English Romantic Poets*, ed. M. H. Abrams (New York, 1960).

9. For this plate see G. E. Bentley, Jr., *William Blake, Vala, Or the Four Zoas* (Oxford, 1963), p. 114. The same author provides a base for Blake discussions in *Blake Records* (Oxford, 1969).

10. See the Richmond Lattimore translation, *The Iliad of Homer* (Chicago, 1964), p. 75 (book I, ll. 605-608).

11. See Northrop Frye, *Fearful Symmetry, A Study of William Blake* (Boston, 1962), pp. 281 and 248.

12. James Joyce, *Portrait of the Artist as a Young Man* (Viking, New York, 1964), p. 253.

13. See Frye, pp. 271-272.

14. G. E. Bentley, p. 157, indicates that "the first fair copy, about 1797 . . . is obviously a fair copy of rough drafts which have not been preserved." Though Blake revised the manuscript through 1804, I am guessing that he began work on it as early as 1795. Erdman's educated guess is that Blake wrote "The Tyger" "between 1790 and late 1792" (Erdman and Bloom, p. 714).

15. David V. Erdman, *Blake, Prophet Against Empire* (Princeton, 1954), p. 180.

Chapter 3

1. *Autobiography of John Stuart Mill*, ed. John Jacob Coss (New York, 1944), p. 104.

2. My text for "Tintern Abbey" is the 1849-1850 *Poetical Works*; for

The Prelude, the edition of 1850. The credibility of that part of my treatment of "Tintern Abbey" based upon punctuation is weakened by our inability to determine what punctuation Wordsworth himself is responsible for in both early and late editions. However, Wordsworth never claimed that he had been misrepresented and his silence on the matter suggests that he was at least not dissatisfied with the 1849-1850 edition in so far as he looked at it.

3. For bibliographical reference to critical comment on "Tintern Abbey" see E. F. Henley and D. H. Stam, *Wordsworthian Criticism, 1945-1964* (New York, 1965). Among the most interesting recent treatments of the poem are Karl Kroeber, *The Artifice of Reality* (Madison, 1964), pp. 87-96, David Perkins, *Wordsworth and the Poetry of Sincerity* (Cambridge, 1964), pp. 204-210, Geoffrey H. Hartman, *Wordsworth's Poetry, 1787-1814* (New Haven, 1965), pp. 26-29, Carl R. Woodring, *Wordsworth* (Boston, 1965), pp. 59-64, Michael G. Sundell, " 'Tintern Abbey' and 'Resignation'," *Victorian Poetry*, V (1967), 255-264, Jean Deubergue, "Time, Space and Egotistical Sublime: The Unity of 'Tintern Abbey'," *Bulletin de la Faculté des Lettres de Strasbourg*, 47 (1969), 203-216, and James A. Heffernan, *Wordsworth's Theory of Poetry: The Transforming Imagination* (Ithaca, 1969). Mary Moorman, *William Wordsworth: A Biography, The Early Years, 1770-1803* (Oxford, 1957), pp. 401-403, has the best account of Wordsworth's version of the conditions under which the poem was written. Albert S. Gérard, "Dark Passages: Exploring Tintern Abbey," *Studies in Romanticism*, III (1963), 10-23, contains the best extended analysis of the poem. He concludes that "Wordsworth was first and foremost concerned with expressing the complex totality of a mood which included both elements of knowledge and of half knowledge" (p. 22). Gérard's essay on "Tintern Abbey" anticipates his conclusions in *English Romantic Poetry: Ethos, Structure, and Symbol in Coleridge, Wordsworth, Shelley, and Keats* (California, 1968).

4. "Dejection: An Ode," *The Poems of Samuel Taylor Coleridge*, ed. E. H. Coleridge (London, 1912), p. 365. All references to Coleridge's poetry cite this edition.

5. For a study of the role of memory in Wordworth's poetry, see Christopher Salvesen, *The Landscape of Memory; A Study of Wordsworth's Poetry* (London, 1965).

6. Woodring, p. 59, writes that "Tintern Abbey" is "not concerned with place. That is, the lines are not in any sense directly connected with Tintern Abbey . . . More nearly it is a poem about 'this delightful stream,' the Wye, and 'this green pastoral landscape' along the river." James Benziger, "Tintern Abbey Revisited," *PMLA*, LXV (1950), 154-162, declares that "to Wordsworth the landscape of the Wye declared the unity of the universe."

7. I suggest this pattern as a speculative abstract which summarizes the general movement of the poet in Wordsworth's poetry as a whole. No one poem presents the complete cycle, though "Tintern Abbey" and *The Prelude* come closest to doing so, and some elements in the movement may be there only by inference.

8. Marshall Suther, *Visions of Xanadu* (New York, 1965), explores many of the possibilities of "Kubla Khan," including this one, and Irene H. Chayes, "Kubla Khan and the Creative Process," *Studies in Romanticism*, VI (1966), 1-21, summarizes this approach.

9. See Chayes, "Kubla Khan and the Creative Process," and Marjorie Hope Nicolson, *Mountain Gloom and Mountain Glory, The Development of the Aesthetics of the Infinite* (Ithaca, 1959).

10. See Gérard, p. 11.

11. See *The Prelude*, VIII, 257-282, 476-494, and 676-686.

12. See Gérard, pp. 10-11.

13. For a history of Wordsworth's attitude toward his audience, see Perkins, VI, pp. 143-175.

14. Gérard concludes, pp. 22-23, that despite the ambiguity of "Tintern Abbey," Wordsworth expresses confidence in and "complete assurance of the benevolence of nature."

15. Moorman writes that "there can be little doubt that Wordsworth's physical suffering during the last two or three years (1799-1802)—his prostrating headaches, the pain in his chest and side, and above all perhaps his sleeplessness—were arousing in him fears that he would not be able to continue with his poetic vocation . . . The future may well have looked black, and depression have been a frequent companion" (p. 539).

16. For comment on Wordsworth's use of incremental repetition, see O. J. Campbell and P. Mueschke, "Wordsworth's Aesthetic Development, 1795-1802," *Essays and Studies in English and Comparative Literature* (Ann Arbor, 1933), p. 32.

17. For a full-length treatment of the relationship between mind and nature in Wordsworth's poetry, see C. C. Clarke, *Romantic Paradox, An Essay on the Poetry of Wordsworth* (New York, 1963), especially pp. 39-53.

18. Hartman, pp. 17-18 and throughout, emphasizes the importance of the moment of the liberation of the imagination.

19. See G. Wilson Knight, "The Wordsworthian Profundity," *The Starlit Dome* (London, 1959).

20. For a focus on this "epic" problem in Wordsworth's career and life, see E. E. Bostetter, *The Romantic Ventriloquists* (Seattle, 1963), pp. 12-81, and Richard J. Onorato, *The Character of the Poet: Wordsworth in "The Prelude"* (Princeton, 1971).

21. Wallace Stevens, *The Collected Poems of Wallace Stevens* (New York, 1957), p. 250.

22. O. J. Campbell, "Wordsworth's Conception of the Aesthetic Experience," *Wordsworth and Coleridge*, ed. E. L. Griggs (Princeton, 1939), comments that "the real subject of this poem is the aesthetic experience" (p. 31). Also see Alexander King, *Wordsworth and the Artist's Vision: An Essay in Interpretation* (London, 1966).

23. See Bostetter, pp. 91-97.

24. See M. H. Abrams, "The Correspondent Breeze: A Romantic Metaphor," *English Romantic Poets: Modern Essays in Criticism*, pp. 37-54.

25. See Gérard, p. 19.

26. *The Notebooks of Samuel Taylor Coleridge*, 1794-1804, ed. Kathleen Coburn (New York, 1957), I, entry 308.

27. For a vivid depiction of William, Dorothy, "Tintern Abbey," and the ravages of time, see E. DeSelincourt, *The Poetical Works of William Wordsworth* (London, 1952), II, 517.

28. See Moorman's account of the role memory and oral composition played in the creation of "Tintern Abbey," referred to in note 3.

Chapter 4

1. M. H. Abrams, "Structure and Style in the Greater Romantic Lyric," *From Sensibility to Romance*, pp. 530-531.

2. See Abrams, p. 533.

3. See Marshall Suther, p. 287, Irene H. Chayes, pp. 1-21, and George Watson, *Coleridge the Poet* (New York, 1966), pp. 117-130. Among recent books on Coleridge that touch on problems of anxiety and creativity, particularly in "Frost at Midnight" and "Dejection: An Ode," are Patricia M. Adair, *The Waking Dream: A Study of Coleridge's Poetry* (New York, 1967), Beverly Fields, *Reality's Dark Dream: Dejection in Coleridge* (Kent, Ohio, 1967), and Walter Jackson Bate, *Coleridge* (New York, 1968). Norman Fruman, *Coleridge: The Damaged Archangel* (New York, 1971), draws heavily on notebooks and psychological analysis to explore at length Coleridge's anxieties about self and creativity.

4. The problem of the date of composition of "Kubla Khan" sometimes seems almost as formidable as the poem itself. E. H. Coleridge seems to accept May 1798 as the approximate date of composition (p. 295). The February 1798 date of "Frost at Midnight" comes from Coleridge himself.

5. Humphry House, *Coleridge* (London, 1953), p. 78.

6. George McLean Harper, "Coleridge's Conversation Poems," *English Romantic Poets: Modern Essays in Criticism*, pp. 144-147.

7. *Collected Letters of Samuel Taylor Coleridge*, ed. E. L. Griggs (Oxford, 1956), IV, 545.

8. House, p. 83.

9. G. Robert Stange, "Introduction," *Coleridge*, The Laurel Poetry Series (New York, 1959), p. 18.

10. Robert Langbaum, *The Poetry of Experience* (New York, 1957), p. 45.

11. Stange, p. 19.

12. Max F. Schulz, *The Poetic Voices of Coleridge* (Detroit, 1963), p. 92. See also Michael Sundell, "The Theme of Self-Realization in 'Frost at Midnight,' " *Studies in Romanticism*, VII (1967), 34-39.

13. House, p. 81.

14. Stange, p. 20.

15. James D. Boulger, "Imagination and Speculation in Coleridge's Conversation Poems," *JEGP*, LXIV (1965), 691-711, asserts that "the Conversation Poems are essentially about the maker and especially the making of poetry." He stresses that "the tensions and contradictions of 'Dejection' . . . are all present in . . . early poems."

16. House, p. 81.

17. See Albert S. Gérard, "The Systolic Rhythm: The Structure of Coleridge's Conversation Poems," *Essays in Criticism*, X (1960), 307-319.

18. For a full discussion of Coleridge's phrase "abstruse researches," see Marshall Suther, *The Dark Night of Samuel Taylor Coleridge* (New York, 1960), Chapter I, "Poetry Versus 'Abstruse Researches,' " pp. 13-24.

19. *The Notebooks of Samuel Taylor Coleridge*, ed. Kathleen Coburn (New York, 1957), I, 330.

20. Schulz, pp. 94-95.

21. For a brief account of the relationship between the fire imagery in "Frost at Midnight" and in "Dejection: An Ode" and for citation of relevant notebook passages, see George Whalley, *Coleridge and Sara Hutchinson and the Asra Poems* (Toronto, 1955), pp. 127-128.

22. House, p. 82.

23. See Suther, pp. 13-24, and *Biographia Literaria*, ed. J. Shawcross (London, 1907), I, 10. Both context and content lead me to equate roughly "Abstruser musings" with "abstruse researches." Boulger (692) "believes the struggle between imagination and abstraction is unending in the Conversation Poems and that . . . the sources of this struggle" are "the permanent contradictions of Coleridge's life and world."

24. *Collected Letters*, I, 183.

25. E. H. Coleridge, *Poems*, p. 240.

26. See Boulger, 709.

27. *Collected Letters*, I, 275.

28. *Collected Letters*, I, 245.

29. See Fruman, *Damaged Archangel*, p. 420.

30. Suther, *The Dark Night*, p. 175.

31. Bostetter, p. 132.

Chapter 5

1. For a history of the critical reception of "Locksley Hall," see William D. Templeman, "A Consideration of the Fame of 'Locksley Hall'," *Victorian Poetry*, I (1963), 81-103. The attitude of Tennyson's contemporaries to his poetry is well represented in *Tennyson: The Critical Heritage*, ed. John D. Jump (New York, 1967).

2. For my text throughout my discussions of Tennyson I use *The Complete Poetical Works of Tennyson*, ed. W. J. Rolfe (Cambridge, 1898). Though undoubtedly *The Poems of Tennyson*, ed. Christopher Ricks (London, 1969) will be the authoritative text for the future, it came too late for frequent citation here.

3. See G. Robert Stange, "Tennyson's Garden of Art: A Study of the 'Hesperides'," *PMLA*, LXVII (1952), 732-743, for a discussion of the east-west, morning-night motif; reprinted in *Critical Essays on the Poetry of Tennyson*, ed. John Killham (London, 1960).

4. The importance of this subject is discussed at length in Ralph W. Rader, *Tennyson's "Maud": The Biographical Genesis* (Berkeley, 1963), especially chapter 3; for a more general critical discussion, see Gerhard Joseph, *Tennysonian Love: The Strange Diagonal* (Minneapolis, 1968).

5. See Paull F. Baum, *Tennyson Sixty Years After* (Chapel Hill, 1948), pp. 240-245, and E. D. H. Johnson, *The Alien Vision of Victorian Poetry* (Princeton, 1952), p. 60.

6. See Lionel Stevenson, "The 'High-Born Maiden' Symbol in Tennyson," *PMLA*, LXIII (1948), 234-243; reprinted in Killham, *Critical Essays*.

7. H. M. McLuhan, "Tennyson and Picturesque Poetry," *Essays in Criticism*, I (1952), 262-282; reprinted in Killham, *Critical Essays*.

8. See R. A. Forsyth, "The Myth of Nature and the Victorian Compromise of the Imagination," *ELH*, XXXI (1964), 213-240.

9. Tennyson's use of the past is discussed by John Kissane, "Tennyson: The Passion of the Past and the Curse of Time," *ELH*, XXXII (1965), 85-109.

10. See E. C. Bufkin, "Imagery in 'Locksley Hall'," *Victorian Poetry*, II (1964), 23.

11. Though unfortunately he hardly touches on the poets, Herbert L. Sussman, *Victorians and the Machines: The Literary Response to Technology* (Cambridge, 1968), begins a literary discussion of "the ringing grooves of change."

Chapter 6

1. Alfred Lord Tennyson, *A Memoir by His Son* (London, 1897), I,

414, indicates that the earliest version of "Merlin and Vivien" was written in February 1856.

2. *Memoir*, II, 366.

3. Gordon Haight, "Tennyson's Merlin," *Studies in Philology*, XLIV (1947), 549-566.

4. See Clyde de L. Ryalls, *From the Great Deep: Essays on Idylls of the King* (Athens, Ohio, 1967), pp. 51-54.

5. Haight, p. 559.

6. *Memoir*, I, 414, 418. The final title appeared in the Miniature Edition of 1870.

7. Both *Memoir*, I, XII, and Haight make it clear that Tennyson identified himself with Merlin: "From his boyhood he had felt the magic of Merlin—that spirit of poetry—which bade him know his power and follow throughout his work a pure and high ideal . . ."

8. Henry Kozicki, "Tennyson's *Idylls of the King* as Tragic Drama," *Victorian Poetry*, IV (1966), 15-20, and William R. Brashear, "Tennyson's Tragic Vitalism," *Victorian Poetry*, VI (1968), 29-49. Brashear's full argument is detailed in *The Living Will: A Study of Tennyson and Nineteenth-Century Subjectivism* (The Hague, 1969).

9. G. O. Marshall, Jr., *A Tennyson Handbook* (New York, 1963), epitomizes the major approach to the poem: "the old story of how even a wise man can be seduced by persistent sexual appeal" (p. 141).

10. Later in the poem (l. 503) Merlin says that I "needs must work my work." For a discussion of the death wish in Tennyson's poetry, see Langbaum, pp. 89-93. For discussion of the ambiguous drives of the hero of "Ulysses," see W. W. Robson, "The Dilemma of Tennyson," and E. J. Chiasson, "Tennyson's 'Ulysses'," both reprinted in Killham, *Critical Essays*, pp. 155-163, 164-173; John Pettigrew, "Tennyson's 'Ulysses'," *Victorian Poetry*, I (1963), 27-45, and Charles Mitchell, "The Undying Will of Tennyson's Ulysses," *Victorian Poetry*, II (1964), 87-95.

11. For general discussion of the problems of allegory in *Idylls of the King*, see, among others, Baum, pp. 176-213, S. E. Burchell, "Tennyson's Allegory in the Distance," *PMLA*, LXVIII (1953), 418-424, F. L. Priestley, "Tennyson's Idylls" (reprinted in Killham, *Critical Essays*, pp. 239-255), J. H. Buckley, *Tennyson, The Growth of a Poet* (Cambridge, 1965), pp. 171-194, R. B. Wilkenfeld, "Tennyson's Camelot: The Kingdom of Folly," *University of Toronto Quarterly*, 37 (1968), 281-294, J. M. Gray, *Man and Myth in Victorian England: The Coming of Arthur* (Lincoln, 1969), and, for the fullest discussion of the poem, John R. Reed, *Perception and Design in Idylls of the King* (Athens, Ohio, 1970).

12. See note 5.

13. Baum, p. 181.

14. See, for example, C. B. Pallen, *The Meaning of the Idylls of the*

King (New York, 1904), pp. 69-75.

15. Baum, p. 181.

Chapter 7

1. See Betty Miller, *Robert Browning, A Portrait* (New York, 1953), p. 187, and William DeVane, *A Browning Handbook* (New York, 1955), p. 248, for an example of the tenuousness of the disagreement. The most recent but not necessarily most illuminating biographical study is Maisie Ward, *Robert Browning and His World*, Volume I, *The Private Face, 1812-1861* (New York, 1968), Volume II, *Two Robert Brownings? 1861-1889* (New York, 1969). W. O. Raymond, " 'The Jewelled Bow': A Study in Browning's Imagery and Humanism," *PMLA*, LXX (1955), 115-131, comments on Browning's association of moon imagery with his wife.

2. See Miller and DeVane as cited above, Browning's own essay on Shelley, Robert Preyer, "Robert Browning: A Reading of the Early Narratives," *ELH*, XXVI (1959), 531-548, and Thomas J. Collins, "Shelley and God in Browning's *Pauline*: Unresolved Problems," *Victorian Poetry*, III (1965), 151-160.

3. See Curtis Dahl, "The Victorian Wasteland," *College English*, XVI (1955), 341-347.

4. I, 7. All quotations from Browning are from *The Works of Robert Browning*, ed. F. G. Kenyon, Centenary Edition (London, 1912).

5. Preyer (reprinted in *Robert Browning, A Collection of Critical Essays*, ed. Philip Drew, Boston, 1966), p. 159.

6. See DeVane's discussion of "Andrea," pp. 244-248. Three recent studies focus on the poem: Paul A. Cundiff, " 'Andrea del Sarto'," *Tennessee Studies in Literature*, 13 (1968), 27-38, Mario L. D'Avanzo, "King Francis, Lucrezia, and the Figurative Language of 'Andrea del Sarto'," *Texas Studies in Literature and Language*, 9 (1968), 523-536, the latter particularly provocative in regard to the perplexed question of Andrea and King Francis' "golden look," and Elizabeth Bieman, "An Eros Manqué: Browning's 'Andrea del Sarto,' " *Studies in English Literature*, 12 (1970), 651-668.

7. See Langbaum, especially Chapter 1.

8. See Park Honan, *Browning's Characters, A Study in Poetic Technique* (New Haven 1961), pp. 156-157.

9. J. Hillis Miller's discussion of Browning in *The Disappearance of God: Five 19th-Century Writers* (Cambridge, 1963), p. 82, emphasizes that Browning "is a huge sea—massive, profound, but, at the same time, shapeless, fluid, and capricious . . . Browning can convey in his poetry an extraordinary sense of the way consciousness flows out through the sense."

10. Roma A. King, Jr., *The Bow and the Lyre: The Art of Robert*

Browning (Ann Arbor, 1957), p. 24. Two recent books elaborate on Browning's artifice and rhetoric: Roma A. King, Jr., *The Focusing Artifice: The Poetry of Robert Browning* (Athens, Ohio, 1968) and David Shaw, *The Dialectical Temper: The Rhetorical Art of Robert Browning* (Ithaca, 1968).

11. Coleridge, p. 364.

12. A recent essay makes the parallels explicit: Burton R. Pollin, " 'Dover Beach' and 'Andrea del Sarto,' " *Victorian Newsletter*, 33 (1968), 58-59.

13. King, *The Bow and the Lyre*, pp. 25-27.

14. See Bloom, *From Sensibility to Romance*, pp. 513-525, and W. J. Bate, "The English Poet and the Burden of the Past, 1660-1820," *Aspects of the Eighteenth Century*, ed. E. R. Wasserman (Baltimore, 1965), pp. 245-264.

15. See Waldo F. McNeir, "Lucrezia's 'Cousin' in Browning's 'Andrea del Sarto,' " *Notes and Queries*, III (1956), 500-502.

16. Honan, pp. 156-157. Honan's excellent remarks on color imagery in the poem are on pp. 191-192.

17. The possible honesty of Andrea's actual relationship with Francis is referred to in DeVane, pp. 247-248.

18. J. Hillis Miller, p. 136.

Chapter 8

1. Originally printed as "Introductory Essay" to a volume of forged letters, *Letters of Percy Bysshe Shelley* (1852). Reprinted as "Browning's Essay on Shelley," *The Percy Reprints*, No. 3, ed. H. F. B. Brett-Smith (Boston, 1921).

2. Mill's comments on *Pauline* appear in Drew, pp. 176-177. See A. R. Jones, "Robert Browning and the Dramatic Monologue: The Impersonal Art," *Critical Quarterly*, 9 (1968), 301-328, and Barbara Melchiori, *Browning's Poetry of Reticence* (New York, 1968).

3. Paul F. Jamieson, "Browning's 'Pictor Ignotus,' " *Explicator*, XI (1952), Item 8.

4. DeVane, p. 156.

5. E. D. H. Johnson, pp. 110-111; J. M. Cohen, *Robert Browning* (London, 1952), p. 36.

6. L. R. Stevens, "Aestheticism in Browning's Early Renaissance Monologues," *Victorian Poetry*, III (1965), 19-24, suggests that the major point of the poem is "that although the aesthetic sensibility is not in itself adequate to provide a meaningful life, it is not necessarily a converse to the meaningful life. The alternatives are not between art and ethics, but between ethics and the lack of ethics" (p. 22).

7. A number of critics have dwelled on Browning's own "success-failure" polarity, among them Betty Miller and Robert Preyer.

8. Identified by some critics as Raphael. See DeVane, p. 156, and *Victorian Poetry and Poetics*, ed. W. E. Houghton and G. R. Stange (Boston, 1959), p. 185.

9. *Percy Reprints*, No. 3, pp. 64-65.

10. *Ibid.*, p. 69.

11. See Langbaum, Chapter 1.

12. See Emery Neff, *Carlyle and Mill* (New York, 1924), p. 180.

13. See Betty Miller, pp. 20-22.

14. See William DeVane, *Browning's Parleyings* (New Haven, 1927), pp. 32, 291.

15. For the "facts" of the poem, see DeVane, *Handbook*, pp. 288-289, and Houghton and Stange, p. 263.

16. Houghton and Stange, p. 263.

17. For a discussion of the role of such imagery in Browning's poetry in general, see J. Hillis Miller, Chapter III.

18. Mrs. Miller, pp. 135-136, emphasizes that Browning himself was hardly an epitome of bold action.

19. See DeVane, *Handbook*, p. 288, and Houghton and Stange, p. 263.

20. *The Poetical Works of Matthew Arnold*, ed. C. B. Tinker and H. F. Lowry (New York, 1950), p. 182. All references to Arnold's poetry cite this edition, though the textual notes in *The Poems of Matthew Arnold*, ed. Kenneth Allott (London, 1967), have been instructive.

Chapter 9

1. For comment on the importance of Wordsworth's influence on Arnold, see U. C. Knoepflmacher, "Dover Revisited: The Wordsworthian Matrix in the Poetry of Matthew Arnold," *Victorian Poetry*, I (1963), 17-26, Leon Gottfried, *Matthew Arnold and the Romantics* (London, 1963), Chapter II, and Paul G. Blount, "Matthew Arnold on Wordsworth," *Studies in Literary Imagination*, I, 1 (1968), 3-11.

2. See *Autobiography*, p. 104.

3. Gottfried, p. 5, makes the point well in general terms when he refers to "Arnold's quandary as a man virtually unable to express his sense of the bankruptcy of Romanticism except in Romantic terms."

4. A. Dwight Culler, *Imaginative Reason: The Poetry of Matthew Arnold* (New Haven, 1965), p. 24.

5. See Gottfried, Chapter V, and William A. Jamison, *Arnold and the Romantics* (Copenhagen, 1958), Chapter VI.

6. On the Coleridge "problem," see Suther, *The Dark Night of Samuel Taylor Coleridge*.

7. Since E. D. H. Johnson, Arnold critics, including Frank Kermode, *The Romantic Image* (London, 1957), Walter E. Houghton, "Arnold's 'Empedocles on Etna,' " *Victorian Studies*, I (1958), and William A. Madden, *Matthew Arnold, A Study of the Aesthetic Temperament in Victorian England* (Bloomington, 1957), have suggested that both Empedocles and Callicles represent aspects of Arnold. Arnold himself probably began the identification game by comparing himself to Empedocles gasping for air. See *The Letters of Matthew Arnold to Arthur Hugh Clough*, ed. H. F. Lowry (New York, 1932), p. 130.

8. W. H. Auden, "Matthew Arnold," *Collected Shorter Poems* (New York, 1950), p. 73, is an example of this line of criticism of Arnold the man.

9. Kermode, p. 19.

10. The importance of this theme in Arnold's poetry has been stressed by many, especially Lionel Trilling, *Matthew Arnold* (New York, 1939). See also, for varied approaches to Arnold's concerns, G. Robert Stange, *Matthew Arnold: The Poet as Humanist* (Princeton, 1957), Fraser Neiman, *Matthew Arnold* (New York, 1968), and David DeLaura, *Hebrew and Hellene in Victorian England: Newman, Arnold, and Pater* (Austin, 1969).

11. Kermode's phrase, p. 13, is that "Empedocles is the Romantic poet who knows enough; Callicles the Romantic poet who does not know enough."

12. See C. B. Tinker and H. F. Lowry, *The Poetry of Matthew Arnold, A Commentary* (New York, 1940), pp. 289-300, Warren D. Anderson, *Matthew Arnold and the Classical Tradition* (Ann Arbor, 1965), pp. 36-47, and Kenneth Allot, "A Background for 'Empedocles on Etna,' " *Essays and Studies by Members of the English Association*, 21 (1968), 80-100.

13. Culler emphasizes a landscape vocabulary to describe "the world" of Arnold's poems and applies the images of the forest glade and the burning plain to his discussion of "Empedocles on Etna" (pp. 157-160). A broader discussion of such imagery appears in Alan Roper, *Arnold's Poetic Landscapes* (Baltimore, 1969).

14. Coleridge, p. 365.

15. Arnold's letter to Clough, March 4, 1848, makes it clear that he had read carefully the *Bhagavad Gita*. See *The Letters of Matthew Arnold to Arthur Hugh Clough*, p. 71.

16. Coleridge, p. 297.

17. Meredith B. Raymond, "Apollo and Arnold's 'Empedocles on Etna,' " *A Review of English Literature*, VIII (1967), 22-32, emphasizes the importance of closely reading Callicles' songs.

18. See Culler, pp. 35-36.

19. Compare Tennyson's:

Much have I seen and known,—cities of men
And manners, climates, councils, governments,
Myself not least, but honor'd of them all . . .
I am a part of all that I have met . . . .

20. Madden, p. 101, writes that " 'Empedocles on Etna' embodies a paradox: it represents the momentary triumph of Arnold's poetic power over his modern self-consciousness in poetry which tells the story of the triumph of that self-consciousness over his muse."

21. See J. Hillis Miller, Chapter V.

Chapter 10

1. See *Dearest Isa: Robert Browning's Letters to Isabella Blagden*, ed. Edward C. McAleer (Austin, 1951), p. 105.

2. *Dearest Isa*, p. 276. Arnold's comment that "Browning's desire that I should republish 'Empedocles' was really the cause of the volume appearing at all" appears in *Letters of Arnold*, I, 431, July 23, 1867.

3. Culler, p. 162.

4. Elizabeth Browning in a letter of May 2, 1853, included in *Letters of the Brownings to George Barrett*, ed. Paul Landis (Urbana, 1958), p. 184, writes, "Have you heard a volume of poems by Dr. Arnold's son ('by A') spoken of in London? There is a great deal of thought in them & considerable beauty. Mr. Lytton lent them to us the other day." "Empedocles" had appeared in October, 1852 (see *The Letters of Matthew Arnold to Arthur Hugh Clough*, p. 123). DeVane, p. 256, indicates that "the second part of *Saul* was probably written during the winter of 1852-3 when Browning began to think of a new volume of poems."

5. Summaries of the "logic" appear in Ward Hellstrom, "Time and Type in Browning's 'Saul'," *EHL*, XXXIII (1966), 370-389, and in David Shaw, "The Analogical Argument of Browning's 'Saul'," *Victorian Poetry*, II (1964), 277-282. A general discussion of Browning's religion is Kingsbury Badger, "See the Christ Stand," reprinted in Drew, pp. 72-95.

6. See James Benziger, *Images of Eternity, Studies in the Poetry of Religious Vision from Wordsworth to T. S. Eliot* (Carbondale, 1962), p. 186, and Derek Colville, *Victorian Poetry and the Romantic Religion* (Albany, 1970).

7. In referring to "Saul" as a Shelleyan poem, Shaw, p. 280, writes that "David's imaginative approach to God combines the Platonic inspiration of waking from 'life's dream' to the day-spring of eternal life with the inner inspiration of a Nonconformist . . . To this Browning also brings a powerful use of the creative imagination, which is probably his most immediate legacy from the Romantic movement."

8. King, *The Bow and the Lyre*, Chapter VI, criticizes "Saul" as if it

were a dramatic monolog to be judged by the standards of unity and character analysis implicit in the dramatic monolog form as generally practiced by Browning.

9. See DeVane, pp. 254-257.

10. Hellstrom, p. 375, writes that "Browning . . . sees both David and Saul as types of Christ. The imagery which surrounds them in the poem is therefore most meaningful if it is seen as typical . . . All the images are related because they point to a center—which is Christ."

11. A. W. Crawford, "Browning's Answer to Empedocles: Browning's 'Cleon,'" *JEGP*, XXVI (1927), 485-490, demonstrates that "Cleon . . . seems to be meant as a sort of companion poem or supplement to Arnold's 'Empedocles on Etna,' and furnished Browning an opportunity to show that Greek culture, at the end as at the beginning, can offer nothing but despair to the longing and inquiring human spirit" (489-490). It seems likely that the second part of "Saul" was a variation of the same reaction.

12. Cohen, p. 39, and Johnson, p. 109, both see David as representative of Browning's "artist-type" and, as has become traditional, Cohen associates David with Browning himself.

13. See Suther, *The Dark Night*, p. 184.

Chapter 11

1. Wallace Stevens, *The Collected Poems of Wallace Stevens* (New York, 1957), pp. 249-250.

Index

Abner, 147, 148

Abrams, M. H., 170 *n*

"Abstruser researches," 48, 50, 54, 57, 61, 175 *n*

Achilles, 136

"Ah! Sunflower," 23

Amy, 119

"The Ancient Mariner," 106, 151, 159

"Andrea del Sarto," 13, 14, 65, 71, 94–108, 110, 113, 114, 118, 119, 123, 146, 161, 162, 163, 164

Apollo, 130, 132, 139, 140, 154

Ariel, 146

Aristotle, 125

Arnold, Matthew: and Coleridge, 45; as critic, 167; "Dover Beach," 98; "Empedocles on Etna," 13, 15, 16, 61, 68, 124–143, 160, 161, 163, 164, 166, 167; preface of 1853, 125; "Rugby Chapel," 63; similarities to Coleridge, 125–126; "To Marguerite," 68, 98, 123; mentioned, 74, 75, 77, 79, 114, 143–147, 162, 165

Art and society: Wordsworth, 39

106, 139; death-in-life, 151; development, 163–164; enervation, 163; eternal language, 47; eye imagery, 22; golden past, 105; hermit, 89; joy, 128, 144; joylessness, 163; Lancelot's lute, 87; landscape as poem, 38; landscape as symbol, 96; landscape, psychological, 131; landscape transformation, 15; landscape, 33, 35, 47, 164, 181 n; light, 163, metaphors of art, 46; nature and Callicles, 135; nature demythologized, 68; nature's degradation, 76; nature worship, 28; nature, 18; marine, 122; moon and gold, 106–107; prison as cage, 86; prison as castle, 86; prison as house, 86; prison as oak tree, 16, 88; prison as tower, 86; prison enclosures, 107; prison-house, 86, 122; prison, 16, 81, 85, 108, 163–164; self-image, 157; storm, 77, 81, 85, 91–93; 148; summary, 163–164; this study about, 11; volcano, 16, 61, 126, 133–134, 138, 140, 163, 164, 167; wasteland, as rhetoric, 97; wasteland poems, 95; wasteland, 96, 104, 106, 148, 164; wind, 23, 130, 163–164

Romantic meditative ode, 12, 44, 62, 63, 64, 71, 75, 83, 90, 101, 104, 158, 159, 160, 165, 170 n

Romantic myth: Blake, 27; created tradition, 157; creative process, 33; Daedalus and Icarus, 23; Daedalus, Vulcan, Hephaestos, 24; golden past, 101–102; ideal poet, 138; illness, two traditions, 128–129; memory, role of, 35; metempsychosis, 126; nature, 68; nature, Victorian attitude toward, 68; nature and poetry, role of, 39; nature as ennobling, 150; prebirth, 133; rebellion of Typho, 138; rebirth, 36; transformation, 137; Wordsworth, 30, 41, 43; Wordsworth's hermit, 32; Wordsworth's poet, 32

Romantic solipsism: egocentricity, 56; mind as internal prison, 164

Romantic structure: circular movement, 45; coalescence of image and form, 57; development, 160, 164–167; development of forms, 158–159; lyric or dramatic, 162; from lyric to dramatic, 78; from ode to monolog, 62; organicism, 46; rationalization, 105–106; subjective or objective, 162; subjective to objective, 163; summary, 164–167; syntax, 33–34; Tennyson, 161; this study about, 11; towards fiction, 167; Wordsworth's epic, 37; See also Romantic meditative ode

Romantic variable lyric: See Romantic meditative ode

Rome, 107

"Rugby Chapel," 63

Sagramore (Sir), 90

Samson, 149

"Saul," 13, 70, 130, 135, 144–155, 162, 163

Shakespeare, William: Henry IV, Part One, 25; mentioned, 84, 90, 103, 109

Shaw, Bernard, 164

Shaw, David, 182 n

Shelley, Percy B.: apostrophied by Browning, 95; as "sun-treader," 162; Browning's essay on, 109,

Fred Kaplan, associate professor of English at Queens College, City University of New York, received his B.A. from Brooklyn College, and his M.A. and Ph.D. from Columbia University. He is a frequent contributor of articles on eighteenth- and nineteenth-century English literature.

The manuscript was edited by Jean Spang. The book was designed by Gil Hanna. The type face for the text is Illumna based on the Electra type designed by W. A. Dwiggins; and the display face is Bembo designed by Arnold Fairbank on a roman face cut by Francesco Griffo in the 15th century.

The text is printed on 60 lb. Nashoba Eggshell paper and the book is bound in Holliston Mills' Kingston and Novelex cloths over binders boards. Manufactured in the United States of America.